306.8742
P428f

From Deadlines to Diapers

DETROIT PUBLIC LIBRARY

SOCIOLOGY & ECONOMICS
CIRCULATING

DATE DUE

MAR - 4 1995

DPL
DISCARD

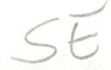

FROM *Deadlines* TO *Diapers*

JOURNAL OF AN AT-HOME FATHER

Mike Perricone

The Noble Press, Inc.
CHICAGO

Copyright 1992 by Michael S. Perricone. All rights reserved.

No part of this book may be reproduced or transmitted in any form or by any means, electronic or mechanical, including photocopying, recording, or by any information storage and retrieval system, without written permission from the publisher.

Printed in the United States of America

Library of Congress Cataloguing-in-Publication Data

Perricone, Mike (Michael S.).
    From deadlines to diapers : journal of an at-home father / Mike Perricone
      p. cm.
    ISBN 1-879360-22-5 (pbk.) : $11.95
    1. Househusbands--United States.   2. Fatherhood--United States.
I. Title.
HQ756.6.P47   1992
    306.874'2--dc20   92-50437
                                                                                 CIP

Noble Press books are available in bulk at discount prices. Single copies are available prepaid direct from the publisher.

The Noble Press, Inc.
213 W. Institute Place, Suite 508
Chicago, Illinois 60610
(800) 486-7737

To Joan

Contents

Before the Beginning   *1*

Pregnancy   *19*

New Parenthood   *45*

Options: Daycare and the Daddy Track   *71*

Bags, Bottles, and Books   *85*

A Father's Job   *109*

The Diaper Diary   *133*

Getting Control   *167*

A Year and a Life   *197*

Epilogue   *219*

Acknowledgments

I'D LIKE TO THANK some of the people who played special roles in the story of Jenny and her dad. Catherine Vanderbeck and Kathy D'Antico provided limitless and invaluable loving support. Byron and Nancy Leonard might be the best friends anyone could ask for. Without the care given to Jenny by Meg, Susie, Effie, and Lisa, I would not have had the time to write. More importantly, they taught Jenny valuable lessons about the nature of friendship.

Steve Duke believed in the "Jenny's Dad" columns, which became the foundation of this book, and committed the Chicago *Sun-Times* to them for a year. Marlene Connor believed in the idea of the book, and spent a year making it happen. Doug Seibold believed in the book, and helped turn it into a better book. And Joan always believed in me. Thank you, all of you.

Before the Beginning

THE EDMONTON OILERS won the 1990 Stanley Cup without Wayne Gretzky, their first championship after trading The Great One to Los Angeles in 1988.

The Oilers also won that Cup without me—the first team to do so since 1977. After fifteen years as a sportswriter, twelve of them covering the Chicago Blackhawks and the National Hockey League for the Chicago *Sun-Times*; after a dozen Stanley Cup playoffs and somewhere around 1,250 NHL games, I turned in my laptop computer to become an at-home father.

Instead of crisscrossing North America from September until June, I devoted my personal 1989–90 season to getting my house (and my life) in order, helping my wife through the final stages of a difficult pregnancy, and helping our daughter through the first stages of her life in this world.

But when Edmonton's Petr Klima scored the winning goal against Boston in triple overtime in Game One of the 1990 Cup final, I wasn't there. When Edmonton captain Mark Messier hoisted the Stanley Cup to his shoulders after Game Five and began the traditional victory lap around the ice in proud-but-sagging old Boston Garden, I wasn't there, either.

Did I miss life on ice? You bet I did.

That 1990 Stanley Cup final was played in two of my favorite cities: Boston and Edmonton. Boston was always my favorite city for visiting old friends, for dining, celebrating, walking, shopping, and absorbing history. Edmonton was one of my favorite cities for piling up frequent flyer mileage.

There is a convention-like atmosphere at the Stanley Cup final, at least among the media and the hockey people not directly involved with the two teams. Everyone swaps rumors and "war stories." Everyone checks out everyone else's travel plans for the series. No one stops working (well, almost no one), and the deadline pressure never ceases, but the work seems lightened by a shared sense of making it through to the end. Even some of the players will share that feeling with you.

And hockey is inhabited mostly by real people, which may differentiate it from some other sports I've covered. Who would not miss a job where you dealt with people of the quality of Doug Wilson, Denis Savard, and Keith Brown every day for ten years or more, and came to think of them as friends? Who would not miss a job that led you to know a Stan Mikita or a Tony Esposito? Who would not anticipate sharing the thoughts of a Wayne Gretzky or a Kevin Lowe during their quest for the Cup? These are all people you would want as your neighbors, whether they played a sport or drove a truck.

Covering any sport involves more than people and championships. The process begins in training camp and moves one day at a time (sometimes one minute at a time) through an endless succession of regular-season games. There are now eighty-four of them in the NHL, beginning in October and ending in April, played from Boston to Los Angeles and from Edmonton to St. Louis. Except for the playoffs, and except for a treasured February stop in L.A., you seldom spend more than one night in any town.

When Earl Weaver retired as manager of the Baltimore Orioles and left baseball, he said: "I'll miss The Game, but I won't miss the games." When Gretzky was once asked about the glamor of life on the go, he said: "My father told me to play hockey so I wouldn't have to get up at six A.M. to work in a factory. So now I get up at five to catch a plane."

Always, there is a plane to catch for the next game. This is what I did not miss about that 1990 Stanley Cup final: shifting scenes from Boston to Edmonton after Game Two meant an eight-and-a-half-hour haul by way of Toronto, if you were lucky enough to get the Air Canada connection; or a nine-hour trek through Salt Lake City, if you landed the Delta connection. Then you'd still have to go through customs. A nine-hour trip should bring you to London or Paris, not Edmonton.

And let's not forget those regular-season trips with seven games in twelve nights, stretching from Quebec City to Calgary, by way of Pittsburgh, Buffalo, Detroit, Minneapolis, and Winnipeg. If you ever long to feel cold, wind-battered, isolated, and depressed, try Winnipeg in January.

The traveling and repetition finally got to me: too much time away covering too many games with too little meaning. No weekends off. Working nearly 100 straight days. Crazy hours leading to crazy eating and drinking habits that could ruin an old stomach (as mine was ruined) or a new marriage (I wouldn't risk it).

And yet . . .

The old wanderlust made a guest appearance in late May of 1992, when the Blackhawks returned to the Stanley Cup final for the first time since 1973. They had never reached the final in the twelve years I covered them. I never got to see the pageant mounted in doomed old Chicago Stadium, possibly the most electrically exciting arena ever built for watching sports. I never got to be the "host writer" at a championship event.

All those pulls were working on me when I went to lunch with some of my old writer friends before the fourth and final game of the Chicago-Pittsburgh series. We swapped memories, lies, and laughs. They marveled at pictures of my daughter. They kidded me about the change in my waistline (twenty pounds slimmer than in my sportswriting days). "You could be a poster child for the benefits of giving up the beat," said one of my old wordsmith friends.

They looked and sounded tired. I knew how relieved they were when the season ended that night; I knew the relief I had felt after the final game of all those nine-month road trips.

So Pittsburgh won another Stanley Cup without me. And much as I enjoyed the visit and the memories, my old sportswriting friends will have to keep on crowding into planes and press boxes without me. I'm busy trying to build this new life for my family, and for myself. I made the choice, and I would make it again.

The Decision

THAT DAY IN JULY 1989, when I drove home with two 40-pound bags of fertilizer in my trunk, I knew there was no longer any doubt.

I was domesticated.

Also in the car were two trays of flowers and two rose bushes for the stamp-sized garden behind our new townhouse.

Every part of my life at home was more important to me now, including flowers. The reasons were sitting in the front right-hand seat of the car: Joan, my wife, and Jenny Rose, our daughter. Jenny actually wasn't due for another five months, but we already had named her, and we felt as if we knew her. We'd been waiting for her a long time.

We didn't realize it then, of course, but we were waiting for her all through those frazzled times in our twenties and thirties, through all those relationships that never worked out for us. We were waiting for her while we settled into our careers, Joan's in business and mine in journalism, and while we settled into our private lives. But our lives weren't really settled, at least not until Joan and I met in April 1986. Both nearing forty, we soon began to feel we had been waiting for each other. We were married just over a year later.

We felt we could make a success of the second half of our lives, but we found it wasn't so easy to unpack all the emotional baggage we carried with us from the first half. When something did get unpacked, it could lead to a round of "Why won't you ever tell me what you're thinking?" and "Why are you always trying to run my life?" All of which made it even more difficult when we began considering the question of a baby.

Our ages didn't give us the luxury of time to think about coming to terms with ourselves, or with our new permanent relationship, before thinking about a family. Time was more pressing for Joan, since the new demands and opportunities our kinder, gentler era has provided for women have not altered biology.

Each reason for having a child seemed balanced by another reason for not having one. Joan feared the disruption of our relationship. I was afraid of being tied down with a child until I was nearly sixty. We both were terrified by starting a family at an age when our parents' child-raising days had been ending.

Then, in August of 1988, Joan was named president of her company. She came downstairs one night and said the promotion meant there would be no time or room for a child.

For about two weeks, we dealt with each other from a distance. With the possibility suddenly taken away, I realized how strongly I felt about having a child. It took months to deal with my anger and come to terms with the loss I felt.

It wasn't easy for Joan, and I didn't make it any easier. She felt she was depriving me of something, and wondered if she were depriving herself as well. Sometimes we both lay in bed looking at the ceiling, thinking about waking up one morning in our fifties and regretting not having a family.

The catalyst for a decision came on a sub-zero night in February 1989, after I had arrived in Edmonton, Alberta, to cover the National Hockey League All-Star Game as the Chicago *Sun-Times*' hockey writer. The night before the game, I went to the movies to see *The Accidental Tourist*. I was upset by the scene where Geena Davis' troubled young son reaches up trustfully to take William Hurt's hand, and the two walk down an alleyway together. It was an experience I thought I would never have: being touched by a child's love and trust. I wasn't sure what I felt as I walked the icy streets back to my hotel room, but I knew it felt bad.

If Joan and I had learned anything in our marriage, it was the importance of talking to each other honestly. We were both feeling regrets and weren't willing to have them haunt our later life.

So we decided we would try to start a family. Since Joan was now past forty, we felt a time limit was necessary. We set the limit for fall 1989, and then we would reassess the decision. Within a month, Joan was pregnant. And then we faced more questions.

My job involved constant travel, and it would not fit with my idea of being a good father. The job had to be changed. Joan had achieved far more earning power than I, so it made no sense for her to give up her job.

I had been a reporter for nearly twenty years, twelve years in my last job. I defined myself in my work. But the travel, the pace, and the repetition had become hard to handle. The job had affected my health in the last few years, and its strains had affected our marriage from the start.

So we reached a decision based on the tilting point in my career, on economic realities, and on the belief that one of us should be home with our baby. I would leave my job and stay home, working independently while providing full-time care. The drop in income would be secondary to the quality of care we wanted to give our child.

We had been waiting a long time for Jenny, and we wanted the best for her. If it would take being domesticated as an at-home father, then that's just what I would do. Jenny was sure to be worth it.

Who We Were

JOAN AND I LIKED to go to Manhattan as children, for the dazzling shows at Radio City Music Hall. But our families crossed different rivers to get there.

Joan was the oldest of seven children (four girls, three boys, spread out over thirteen years), in a robust Irish family that filled a large house in Ridgewood, New Jersey. Dr. James Vanderbeck, who died in 1987 after a heartbreaking struggle with Alzheimer's Disease, was an obstetrician and surgeon, a skilled card and pool player, and a scratch golfer. And headstrong (a Dutch forebear produced the family name). Catherine Vanderbeck, as far as anyone can tell, is probably a saint.

The Vanderbeck home had trees on the lawn, a loyal family dog, Dr. Vanderbeck's office adjacent to the kitchen, a new car in the driveway, and a swingset in the back yard where Joan and her best friend, Sharon, would swing and sing songs by the hour. Joan's mom essentially ran a small hotel with nine permanent residents, including three boys who liked to climb out windows and hang from tree branches or skitter across the roof. The Vanderbecks would become ardent Kennedy Democrats.

My first neighborhood in Brooklyn dead-ended at one of the huge low-income housing projects put up in the years following World War II. We had a ground-floor apartment in a brick six-flat that had probably been fairly deluxe at one time. My parents, Steve and Rose, had grown up in big families during the Depression; so had Joan's parents, though they were a bit older.

My mother was a secretary in a factory. My father had been too interested in playing baseball on the Brooklyn sandlots to finish high school. After getting married, he worked on the machinery in the same factory as my mother. They didn't own a car until 1956. Work was what my father did most of the time. That was what you were supposed to do in the blue-collar 1950s, even if it meant adding a part-time job at night and on weekends, even if it meant you couldn't see much of your family. My parents were hardworking Eisenhower Republicans, who would become very disappointed Nixon Republicans (my mother cast a surprisingly enthusiastic vote in 1984 for Walter Mondale and Geraldine Ferraro—mostly for Geraldine Ferraro).

School was the focus of childhood for Joan and me.

Joan, who always knew her own mind, wanted to go to boarding school at the age of nine, and she did: the School of the Holy Child, on rambling, verdant grounds in Suffern, New York. She returned home at sixteen to finish high school, then studied political science at Marquette University in Milwaukee.

For me, it was the New York City public school system—in those years, still a thriving marketplace of ideals and possibilities. There was even a destination when I decided I wanted to be an engineer: Brooklyn Technical High School, one of New York's five rigorous "special high schools," with entry by competitive examination. On my first day as a ninth-grader, the newcomers (it was then an all-boys' school) were packed into the 3,000-seat auditorium. The dean of students told each of us to look at the boy in front, the one behind, the one on the left and the one on the right. Of the five of us, we were told, two would not make it through. I spent the next four years making sure I made it through.

But I didn't make it through college as an engineer. I left Rensselaer Polytechnic Institute in Troy, New York, after two years, which eventually cost me my draft deferment. In early 1971, that generally meant Destination: Saigon. But I flunked the pre-induction physical exam, perhaps the most important test of my life, because of congenital health problems. Joan didn't have to face the draft, of course, but her brothers did. Jim, the oldest boy, was then extending his own tour in Vietnam so Jack and Tom wouldn't have to go.

I wound up back at RPI, essentially majoring in sports at the campus radio station. Broadcasting was my new ambition. My professional entry-level job was as a weekend newscaster, first at a station in Troy and later in Albany—where I had a microscopic role in the post-Watergate fallout. President Ford pardoned Richard Nixon during my Sunday-morning shift at WROW, and I broke the news to Dick Rosenbaum, chairman of the New York State Republican Party. He was stunned. He asked for a moment or two to take in the news, then was forthright and quotable (some years later, he became a member of the GOP national committee).

I was trying to earn a living by piecing together part-time jobs in those days, including a night job in the sports department of the *Times Record* (circulation: 40,000) in Troy. I paired up with one of the full-time sportswriters to do a "Woodward-and-Bernstein" investigative number on a promoter who was promising an American Basketball Association franchise for the area—if the investors would build an arena and let him handle their money. We may not have run him out of town, but he did a fast fade—and I was soon offered a full-time job. By the fall of 1974, I had a new career.

Joan moved to Chicago in 1971, because she liked the city. Her jobs started out small, but they couldn't contain her capabilities, her personality, and her energy. Her big break came in 1977, when Don Borzak interviewed her for a job with his web-offset printing company.

"Somebody must have told her to make eye contact, because she just stared at me the whole time, and I was pretty uncomfortable," Don said. "She wasn't overly qualified technically for the job we hired her for. But she just kept doing more than what we asked her for. She just kept taking things on. Saying I'm happy we hired her would be the understatement of the year. Any year."

My big break also came in 1977, when I came to Chicago for a new job, jumping to a newspaper that sold more than 625,000 papers every day and more than 750,000 on Sunday. On July 5, 1977, feeling like Clark Kent when he began *his* career at a great metropolitan newspaper, I worked my first day at the Chicago *Sun-Times*. Instead of being a sportswriter, I was a now a Sportswriter.

That's what I was, and who I was, until I met Joan.

How We Met

1986.

Joan and I lived about a dozen blocks from each other on the North Side of Chicago. We moved in the most different circles. We were destined for separate and nonintersecting lives. Until her friend Don Borzak took matters in hand.

After hiring Joan, Don had watched her rise to prominence over eight inspired years. He knew that Joan needed to meet someone special, a year after she had gone through a divorce. So he wrote and placed a personal ad in the April 1986 issue of *Chicago* magazine—unknown to Joan.

Chicago was in my mailbox on a Sunday morning in March when I returned from a road trip with the Chicago Blackhawks. It would pass some time until I had to go back to work that afternoon. Thumbing distractedly through the magazine, I discovered the personals section.

Don's ad had an irresistible "hook:" replies were asked to name their favorite book.

On a yellow legal pad, using my best former-engineering-student lettering, I printed a full-page reply, my first ever to a personal ad. I used about half the page on lists of favorite books in different categories, since I couldn't be held down to just one favorite.

The answer came a week later, with a message on my answering machine. Her voice was clear, strong, graceful, obviously imbued with education and character. She spoke in complete sentences.

We talked a few times on the phone in the next week or so, the "Who are you?" conversations that can be so strained and halting. But Joan was gracious, interesting, and always interested in what I had to say. We interrupted one conversation when Joan said she had to drive her mother home; she said she would call back later, and she did. I believed I would be meeting one of the nicest and most intelligent women I had ever known.

There was one problem in the way of our meeting: the National Hockey League playoffs were just beginning. But the Blackhawks, whom I had covered for nine mostly mediocre years, lost meekly and quickly in the first round to Toronto. After the post-mortems on the Hawks, there was time to set a date.

The Ballad of Narayama is Shoei Immamura's poetic film about the struggle for existence "some 100 years ago in northern Japan." One of Joan's favorite films, it was playing at the Music Box Theater, near the midpoint between our homes. We would meet there.

I stood in front of a movie poster feeling self-conscious and poorly dressed. Though I usually dressed well when I was working, I often misfired on "casual." On this chilly night, along with a colorless corduroy sport coat, I was wearing the shapeless hat that had led one of the younger Blackhawk players to dub me "Inspector," as in Clouseau.

Across the street came a woman whose posture and manner made her look taller than she was. She was wearing jeans, and a sweater bold in color and pattern. Her stride was long and purposeful. Her nose was aquiline, her cheekbones were high, her black hair was pulled straight back. To me, her whole aura was aristocratic.

"She must have been a model once," I thought. "I'm probably in over my head here. Well, let's make the best of it and see what happens."

We must have said the usual things in introduction, but I don't remember. As we took our seats, I asked if there was anything I could get for her, but she said she had already had dinner.

"I had some cherry juice," she said. "That's all I wanted. I was a little nervous."

We focused on the film, which depicts a great deal of, uh, earthy behavior ("You could really only describe it as 'rutting,'" Joan said at a much later time. "I didn't remember the movie being like that. I sat there wondering what you were thinking about me for dragging you in to see a movie like that on our first date.")

After the film, we took her car to a spot in the neighborhood for some pizza. We talked about traveling. Joan told me about Scotland. I told her about Alaska. She was as interested in listening as she was in talking, and she was a good listener. No one had ever listened to me the way she did.

As we walked back to her car, I slipped my arm around her

waist. Before she got into her car, she said, "I'd like to give you a hug."

She was a kind of woman I had never met before.

On our second date, we went to a library to hear three authors read from their work. We went to museums. We looked at flowers in the park.

We were married fourteen months later, sheltered from a soft rain by the trees in the Shakespeare Gardens beside Howes Chapel, on the Northwestern University campus in Evanston. Don was one of three friends present at the private ceremony; later, back in the city, he arranged a horse-and-carriage tour for us. We told our families of the wedding the next morning, phoning from our hotel room in downtown Chicago. Joan's mom cried with happiness. My parents were equally delighted, though I think they were mostly relieved that, pushing forty, I was finally married. I think I may have felt the same way.

Real life was beginning.

Making It Work

WERE WE COMPLETELY DIFFERENT?

Joan thought so, after we had attended a multi-media performance called "The Siege of Stalingrad." She was absorbed and moved; I was distracted and dubious.

"Sometimes I wonder about us," she said in despair. "We seem to be completely different in so many ways." And for some reason, our differences often went toe-to-toe in the car.

I was perfectly happy to drive in silence; if Joan asked what I was thinking, I could drive her to distraction by reporting: "Nothing." Or, if we had had some recent disagreement, she might become upset, thinking I was angry at her.

We had a classic blowup during our honeymoon tour of Ireland. With a gravel-spitting turn to take Joan's "suggestion" of a shortcut, I plunged us into a maze of narrow country lanes.

I drove blindly for half an hour, more furious by the second, while Joan continually suggested stopping for directions. She couldn't prevent herself from laughing. I've never come closer to taking a poke at her. Finally, I slammed on the brakes at a gas station, slammed the door as I left the car, stalked across the road, and found out the town we wanted was just a mile or two away. Joan was still laughing when I got back to the car. We probably weren't very different from many newly married couples—except that, starting a marriage in our forties, we'd had a lot more time to become set in our ways.

Joan was the communicator. If something was going on for her, she told me about it. If something was going on for me, she wanted to know about it. If something was going on with us, she wanted to get at it. Right away—sometimes before I even realized anything was going on.

I was the shrugger. If something was going on—with me, with Joan, with us—I would shrug, try to ignore it, hope it would go away, and try to go on to something else. I didn't want to deal with an emotional issue if there was a way to deflect it. I felt as if every mistake I had ever made was the result of losing control of some emotion—my temper, my impatience, my anger, my obstinacy, my fear.

If I was honest, I had to admit that emotions were a frightening mystery to me. And I would try a cover-up until they burst out. I scrupulously avoided anything approaching an argument—but if we got near one, Joan could make me nuts by being able to separate herself from her own distress and mine, speaking calmly and rationally while I sputtered and groped.

Joan was the planner, abhorring unstructured time the way nature abhors a vacuum. She could think seriously about where she wanted to be in five years or ten years. I was the postponer. If we had an open evening, I'd postpone a decision about it until—well, that evening. Joan was the cleaner, meticulous about a neat home. As for housework, I abhorred the vacuum.

Joan loved being with people; the bigger the party, the more she loved it. Generally, the one thing I liked better than going to a party was not going to a party. Joan could clearly read emotional signs, in herself and others, where most people could see nothing but fog. She could be startlingly effective with people, socially or professionally, simply by listening to them. But those skills could be discomfiting when focused on me. Sometimes I felt I might punch a wall if I heard "What are you thinking?" or "What are you feeling?" one more time. Yes, I was a communicator, too—but professionally, not personally.

Professionally, we worked similarly: well-organized, in control, taking responsibility to a fault, working long hours, ultra-serious about details—in short, highly demanding of ourselves. Joan largely led her personal life the same way, but when I wasn't working, my phone was off the hook.

To Joan, life was champagne: a bubbly celebration. To me, it was scotch or beer, and hold the metaphor. How could we hope to keep this marriage going?

Being an "older couple" had to help. We were honest, with ourselves and each other. We listened to each other, and paid attention. I've never met a person more honest than Joan, in her life and in her work. I like to think I'm honest about myself; I tried hard to judge my faults objectively, tried hard to use the same standards on myself that I used in reporting.

It took this self-appraisal to make a difference for me: I admired the way Joan could stay cool when I turned red-hot. I marveled at her ability to understand herself and her feelings so completely that she could make a conscious decision about when to act on them and when not to. She could handle virtually any touchy situation with sensitivity and skill. When you speak to Joan, you know you are being heard.

Joan told me I had instinctive skills as a listener. But I had also spent half my life interviewing people and listening to their answers. I did try to be flexible. I wanted to do what worked, and I was willing to change to make things work.

Joan's flexibility grows out of her amazing empathy. After our Ireland blowup, over dinner, she began laughing about the incident again. Then she explained my point of view more clearly than I had seen it myself.

"Here you've been driving this whole trip, doing everything backward," she said, "shifting with the other hand, driving on the other side of the road, navigating these crazy narrow roads where I would have gotten us lost or in a wreck. You finally get to drive on a regular highway and relax—and I get you to take a shortcut and suddenly we're lost. No wonder you were mad."

By then, I was laughing, too.

Pregnancy

The Wait

COMING TO KNOW EACH OTHER had been a series of mostly pleasant discoveries for Joan and me. But before we could start to know who our baby would be, we had to wait through four of the worst days of our lives.

Joan was about ten weeks pregnant for our hospital appointment on Tuesday, May 9, 1989. We met with Beth Fine, a genetic counselor at Illinois Masonic Hospital, for another explanation of the prenatal test, Chorionic Villus Sampling (CVS), that Joan would undergo. The presentation was clear and direct; the procedure was complex. In fact, it was a little scary. In any invasive prenatal test, there is a small but measurable risk of miscarriage; for this test, it was about one in 100.

But we wanted the CVS for two reasons. First, Joan was over forty; in medical terms, as a first-time mother at that age, she was termed an "elderly primigravida." There is a dramatic rise in Down's Syndrome, up to one child in thirty, when mothers give birth after age forty. While children with Down's Syndrome need attentive care and special education, they often are loving, happy children who offer special rewards. But we wanted to know if we needed to prepare ourselves for a special child.

Second, and most important, we were frightened by a condition called Fragile X Syndrome, which is present in Joan's family history. Fragile X is one of the most common genetic defects, carried in about one of 850 people; it is one of the leading causes of mental retardation, affecting one of 1,000 males and about one of 1,600 people overall, but it has been among the least understood genetic problems until recent years.

A defect passed on in the X chromosome has a wide and puzzling range of effects, but it can lead to profound retardation in male children. The effect on females is less clearly understood; at the time we had the test, it was thought that females were basically unaffected.

It was a sunny spring afternoon when we walked into the hospital, but the sunshine didn't warm us. Beth, an earth mother in a lab coat, was helpful, comforting, and understanding. Then came the doctors and the examination room.

In any clinical procedure, the examinee is usually made to feel like a dope. Joan was given a sort of paper jumper, open at the back as are all hospital garments. The paper jumper replaced the clothing on the lower half of her body. I got a stool next to the examination table, to watch and stay out of the way.

For the CVS test, a woman reports with a full bladder so there is pressure on the uterus. When Joan got onto the table, one of the three doctors present asked how she felt.

"I'm nervous," she said, always honest. "And I have a full bladder."

"Well, I'm not nervous," the doctor announced. "And I don't have a full bladder." We weren't surprised when things deteriorated from there.

The CVS involves taking a sample of tissue from the outside of the placenta from among the chorionic villi, which look like long, slender fingers or tendrils. Taking the sample internally, and not piercing the abdomen with a syringe, requires a clear path through to the uterus, as mapped by ultrasound pictures projected onto a monitor.

Joan was having contractions, which are normal throughout pregnancy, but the sample couldn't be taken until they stopped. It might take hours, with the radiologist continually smearing lubricating jelly on Joan's abdomen and applying a sound gun that looks like an oversized electric shaver with a handle. This was the last appointment, we were told, and the team was prepared to wait as long as necessary.

So we waited, and the ambience descended to a level where I thought the doctors would send out for pizza and beer. Joan gathered her dignity and strode back to the dressing room. I followed, feeling like a dope.

We suspected the nurse had said something during our absence, because when we returned another radiologist took over. The new man knew I was a sportswriter and began talking sports to break the ice. I didn't get a chance to make my little speech about this being a routine procedure for them but a stressful experience for us. I still felt like a dope.

It took nearly two hours to get the sample; we probably would not get the results until the following week. The chromosome mapping in the test results would be definite for Down's Syndrome, with indications of Fragile X. We also would learn the sex of the baby if we wanted to know. A boy would mean further tests and further concerns for Fragile X. We wanted to know.

Beth told us she would press for results by Friday, and she would call if she heard anything over the weekend. So we waited.

We had seen our baby for the first time on the ultrasound monitor: a little peanut shape with an astounding heartbeat that the sonar displayed as a pulsating dot. We also got a black-and-white picture of our little peanut taken from the monitor. After our first excitement, we found it too hard to look at the picture.

I had to leave the next day for Calgary to cover the final game of the Blackhawks' playoff series against the Calgary Flames. I wasn't very enthusiastic, but I did my job and returned the following morning. We waited.

Late Friday afternoon I was at my desk at the newspaper, trying to work and shut out the world. My phone rang. It was Joan's secretary, and her voice broke as she told me Joan wanted to speak to me. It felt like bad news.

"Beth called," Joan said through tears. "She said the chromosomes are normal and it's a girl."

I felt like shouting at the sky. It was hard to keep my work face on. Joan said Beth told her the people in her department had celebrated the news with champagne.

We had a different way to celebrate. We had chosen names for both a boy and a girl: it would be Jenny, after the song "Jenny Rebecca" that Joan had first heard sung by Mabel Mercer. And Rose, for my mother.

Our little girl's name was waiting for her. Now we could look at our picture of Jenny, and wait for her to grow.

Through Her Eyes

ON A PERFECT SUMMER AFTERNOON in Chicago, a shiny little toddler was out for a walk with her thirtyish mom and dad. She held hands with both parents as they crossed Wacker Drive at Wabash Avenue, stopping on the median in front of the fountain.

The little girl was thrilled by the falling, splashing water. Her parents, who might have walked right past the fountain if they had been alone, stopped and took the time to share their daughter's interest and join in her delight. They seemed happy to take part in the wonder of her discovery.

When Joan and I were expecting Jenny, I would stop and watch scenes like the one at the fountain, smiling and walking away almost light-headed with anticipation. Fortunately for me, no one ever took exception to my smiling at them and their children. When I happened on these scenes, I always remembered a conversation I had several months before Joan and I reached our decision to start a family.

I asked my friend Doug Wilson, whom I had known from his first days as a defenseman with the Chicago Blackhawks in 1977, what he liked so much about his four children.

"Seeing the world through their eyes," he said. "And their innocence."

And I began to understand what he meant. But I also began to see that there can be a drive to make children see the world through our eyes, and not through theirs.

In a breakfast restaurant on a Sunday morning, Joan and I noticed a big table with a large family seated around it. In one chair was a little boy with his head down, trying hard to keep from crying but not succeeding.

"You did something wrong," his father was telling him sternly, "and I scolded you. There's no reason for you to cry. Stop crying."

The little fellow seemed to have good reason to cry, after being disciplined right in front of grandma and grandpa, other children and other grownups, the whole restaurant.

Whatever he had done wrong, it seemed like the little fellow was put in an impossible situation. He was miserable but he wasn't allowed to express his misery—and he was being told he wasn't even entitled to feel miserable. He was being told he had to see things his father's way, and his own way wasn't just wrong, it didn't even count.

That message seemed very different than trying to teach a child what kind of behavior might be appropriate in a social setting like a restaurant. Joan and I weren't sure what kind of lesson the boy would take from that family breakfast, but we were sure he would remember it for a long time.

We were sure another restaurant meal would be memorable for a young adolescent girl we saw at our favorite neighborhood place on Chicago's near west side, soon after that sad breakfast.

The girl was beginning to see herself as a young woman, and she had to be pleased by the way that view was being affirmed by her father from across the small table. He might have been a divorced father enjoying a weekend visit with his daughter; there was that sense of trying to catch up on what was happening in her life.

But her father was deeply interested in her thoughts and her feelings. He was talking to her as a person, and she obviously loved being treated as a person. If she was feeling just a bit self-conscious, it seemed like a tingly, exciting self-consciousness. Her father thought enough of her to want to know how she saw the world, through her own eyes.

When I began to think about raising a child, my first consideration was to have someone to leave behind me, to carry on for me, and obviously to do things the way I wanted them done. But once Joan and I knew that Jenny was on her way, my feelings and my outlook began to change. It didn't seem right to think of Jenny as someone whose entire life I could control and direct. As I watched the girl and her father at the next table, I hoped that Jenny and I would enjoy each other as people, not just as father and daughter.

Jenny would have her own life to live, probably sooner than I might expect or even like. Our responsibility was to help make that life as full as it could be. Would we direct her every move in little circles, like a radio-controlled toy boat? Or would we teach her as much as we could, then trust her to judge the winds for herself?

I knew our Jenny would sail her own course. I wanted her to have the best boat and the best sails we could give her.

"Daddy Did It"

MY NEW HEROES were the people who brought us paint rollers and latex interior paint.

When I was growing up in the 1950s, almost nobody in Brooklyn painted an apartment. Rents were low, and it was easier and less aggravating to move to a new place. Remember oil-based paints that left a mess, paint brushes that left a trail, turpentine that left a sting and a smell? And don't forget those fighting words when the painting was done: "You missed a spot!"

Times have changed, bringing relief to fathers everywhere.

Painting Jenny's room was part of the overhaul for our house as we prepared for Jenny's arrival. It was the first time I had painted anything since college, when five of us got our new place ready while going through more beer than paint. This time I was alone, and the beer had to wait until the job was done. This time, the job was a lot neater, too.

But the overhaul never seemed to end. A full-time mom often complains that her role devolves to being a full-time chauffeur. But a full-time dad must be prepared to become a general contractor and full-time handyman.

The job began during the summer, as we planned to rearrange the rooms. My office at the back of the second floor would become Jenny's room. My desk, books, and files had to move down the hall to coexist with the guest/TV room. That meant Joan's desk had to move to our bedroom on the third floor. It also meant Joan's desk had to change finish, from oak to mahogany, for a better match with the furniture.

Moving the desk upstairs took the better part of an afternoon with the help of a friend. Refinishing the desk took the better part of a week and enough sanding to last me a lifetime. But the work was just starting.

Joan and I both love books. We can't part with them. That means we have to move them. My books filled nearly a dozen boxes after they had been emptied from six bookcases—and five of the bookcases were more than six feet tall. The books and bookcases had to move to my new office space, along with my desk. The desk had once been our dining room table. It was more than six feet long and the top was solid oak. Moving the other way, into Jenny's room, was Joan's old birdseye maple dresser, which didn't weigh much more than half a ton.

We planned to have a moving company come in for a couple of hours and do the job. I kept delaying making the call. Finally, I figured out why: my masculinity was on the line here. I didn't want to pay someone else to move my own furniture around in my own home. But money, I realized, was secondary to male ego. I could not stand there, a healthy man without a regular job, and watch other men sweat, grunt, and lift.

So one morning, about 10:00 A.M., I began lifting, grunting and sweating. When I finished at 4:00 P.M., I had a sore back, two rearranged rooms, and a startled wife. And a sense of peace with myself.

But the projects never ended. Pregnant women experience a phase called "the nesting instinct," when they become obsessed with tasks like reorganizing all their closets. In fact, we did rearrange Joan's big closet, with a redesigning by one of those high-tech closet companies.

Perhaps parallel with the nesting instinct, this expectant dad developed "the caulking instinct."

We had had exasperating heating problems since buying our new home, and I became obsessed with sealing and caulking every gap and possible source of cold air I could find. Joan called me "the Mad Caulker." I caulked window frames, baseboards, and shingles. I couldn't stop. I taped over every seam I could reach in the sheet-metal ductwork growing out of our furnace, trying to seal the system. I was determined our house would be warm and tight for Jenny's winter arrival.

The projects made up a long list, from adjusting the gas flame in the stove, to building shelves in the garage, to putting curtains on the glass panels in the back wall of our dining room, to "assembling" Jenny's changing table (does anything made in the USA ever fit together?), and caulking, caulking, caulking. I always felt as if I had forgotten something, though I constantly scavenged hardware stores for ideas and gimmicks.

But I was proud of Jenny's room, those pale lilac walls that matched the color of one of the big, finger-painted flowers in the drapery. I was itching to brag about that even seam between the lilac walls and white ceiling, and about the wicker bookshelves that I repainted white.

Someday, when she was aware of her surroundings, I hoped that Jenny would take delight in that room. And I hoped she might someday ask how it came to be that way, so I could tell her: "Daddy did it."

Joan's Pregnancy

JOAN GAVE HERSELF some funny nicknames during her pregnancy: Tubby McGonagle, Rotunda Sneaker, Minnie LaBelcha. The joke wore off as time wore her down. It wasn't funny to watch her struggling for breath as she climbed a flight of stairs or just walked to the car. "People have been telling me to slow down all my life," she said. "It took getting pregnant to make me do it."

Joan tried to work at her office through Thanksgiving, but fatigue drove her home a week earlier. She still tried to stay connected by fax machine and an extension of her office phone, both of which had been installed in our bedroom.

But after she had a series of chest pains that frightened everyone and defied diagnosis, her executive team sent her a fax letter telling her she was cut off from all but the most critical business information, and all but "How are you feeling?" telephone calls. When Joan read, "Jenny needs you more than we do," she cried. And she admitted she was relieved.

"I take my career seriously, and it was hard to let go of my responsibilities," she said. "I've never let up before. I always felt I should do more, I should work harder. But now I had a difficult adjustment. I was critical of myself. I'd be dragging, and feeling like I should be doing more. Then two days later I would feel better and realize I just hadn't had enough to give. I never wanted to let up. But when you're pregnant, you don't have any choice. You have to let up."

Pregnancy is a continual surrender on one principle after another. Joan has always been an elegant dresser, even in jeans and a sweater. By the last few months of pregnancy, she spent most of her time in sneakers and a plain gray sweatsuit (sweatshirt, size XXL; pants, size XL). She practically shuddered when she tried them on, but soon she actually was leaving the house in her sweats. "They're the most comfortable clothes I have," she said.

It wasn't the sweats that had people staring at her. At least men seemed self-conscious, if not embarrassed. But women seemed to be sizing her up, coolly and openly, thinking, "Oh, look at YOU, honey!"

"Hasn't anybody ever seen a pregnant woman before?" Joan said at one point. But people seemed not to see Joan at all whenever she was having trouble getting through a crowded space, whether in a restaurant or a department store. People seemed dedicated to bumping her and cutting her off.

"I feel like punching somebody," she said more than once.

In the first three months, Joan probably wanted to punch me more than anyone else. I was still traveling in my sportswriting job, and I was gone more than I was home from March until June. She was alone to fight the battle of her changing body, alone with the debilitating nausea and the hollowing fatigue. "I feel like an alien has taken over my body," she said. "I feel like I have a terminal disease."

Except for her growing belly, Joan looked and felt more normal in the second trimester. And she began feeling wiggles inside, startling her at first but bringing joy with the realization that Jenny was beginning to move. We felt like a family—a growing family. Joan and Jenny seemed bigger each day.

But in the third trimester, pain outpaced growth. Joan's hands and feet swelled, sometimes achingly, and she had long since had to take off her wedding ring. She couldn't sleep. She couldn't breathe. She couldn't walk far but she couldn't stand in one place. She couldn't sit comfortably long enough to get involved in a book, and she didn't have the concentration to read much, even if she could sit. Her bladder needed constant emptying. Her digestive tract backed up and packed up. She had heartburn that made her gasp and hemorrhoids that made her cry. And her emotions were scraped raw by the endless waiting in the final weeks.

Joan's doctor said there was no way to tell whether her age had increased her difficulties, because "there just isn't enough data on first-time pregnancies past the age of forty." Joan didn't care much for being labeled an "elderly primigravida." And she was not sentimental when someone told her she would miss being pregnant.

"It's worth every minute of being pregnant for that adorable baby," Joan said. "But I'm not going to miss being pregnant. It's not being fat, or that your clothes don't fit. It's a matter of trying to find a balance with your body and all the new limitations. For the first time in your life, you can't operate on what you've always known about yourself and your body. People can't know how you feel, and they expect you to perform like yourself. But even more important, I always expected to perform like myself, but I couldn't."

We never doubted that Jenny was worth all of this, and more. We also agreed we both were too old to go through this again.

Kitchen Trauma

WHEN I WAS GROWING UP, I read a lot of books and I played a lot of baseball. I even read a lot of books about baseball. But I never cooked. I could handle a fly ball, but not a frying pan. When I was single, in my thirties, in a North Side condo decorated in Contemporary Tornado, I made steaming breakfasts of whole wheat toast and instant coffee. I opened a great can of tuna. I could turn gourmet by sliding a steak into the toaster oven and carefully selecting "broil," adding the finishing touches with six or eight carefully aged and selected beers.

That was before: before Joan, before marriage, and before Jenny.

When Joan and I were getting to know each other, she was aghast that I didn't know the difference between those two commingled Chicago chains, Jewel and Osco: they often stand side by side, and I was never sure which was the drugstore and which was the supermarket.

At least Joan was sympathetic about my anxiety attacks when she began taking me on safari for groceries in places I had never seen before. I discovered all sorts of unusual vegetation, and I got straight on which store sold the food.

What an education! What a change from burger-and-bar-stool days, and those post-midnight runs to bright-light, all-night convenience store outposts for baloney and cheese and rye bread. Real food was a revelation. In fact, there were two revelations about real food: eating it and preparing it. I was totally unprepared for the summer night in 1989 when we chopped all that green stuff in the Cuisinart.

It seemed like a great idea. Joan was about five months pregnant. I was in the process of planning to leave sportswriting on the way to becoming an at-home father.

We wanted to boost our batting average on salads and vegetables, which often wound up suffering long slumps in our refrigerator. The plan was to get all this healthy vegetation chopped up and sorted into plastic bags, so we could parcel it out for daily salads and still keep it fresh. It was Joan's idea, of course. (And Joan's Cuisinart, if you hadn't guessed.)

I also needed kitchen practice, since our plan was to use the Cuisinart to make fresh baby foods once Jenny came along. I would be the hands-on homebody, so it made sense to get to know my way around this gizmo with the sinister-looking blades.

We opened the trapdoor in the top of the machine and began feeding green stuff into it. Lettuce. Celery. Cucumbers. Onions. Radishes (OK, so it wasn't all green). Jam it in, hold down the cover, hit the switch: over and over and over, adding a step to wipe our eyes from the onions.

After about six hours of it, I was ready to be farmed out. I couldn't take the pressure. My nerves were shot. I had the shakes. Especially when I looked at the clock and the clock said we'd only been chopping vegetables for thirteen minutes. What a lie.

If a baseball bat had been handy, I would have swung it through a wall. Instead, I grabbed a beer and bolted for the back yard to calm down. My future in food preparation looked dark, indeed.

Joan finished the chopping solo, then came outside to pat me on the shoulder and make some understanding noises. She calmed me down enough for me to go back inside and finish bagging the ready-made salad with her. It was a hard lesson to learn.

Kitchen. Cuisinart. Vegetables. Plastic bags. Chopping, chopping, chopping. If this was to be my new reality, I wanted back my old life on the run. Having a flight canceled in February in Buffalo was a carnival compared to this kitchen ordeal. Having a French-speaking operator cut off your phone call from Quebec City was nothing compared to cutting up cucumbers. I wanted to go out to O'Hare for a while just to relax in a calm, familiar atmosphere.

The old days had been an escape from this sort of ordinary business of everyday life. I hadn't had to think about it, except to laugh about it. Chopping vegetables? Ha! Other people did that, not me. "Sorry, I'm too busy. Don't have time. See you later, I have to catch a plane. I'll be gone for a week. Five cities. I'll call you. Can you pick me up at the airport when I get back, or should I take a cab home?" Escape. That's what my old life amounted to.

Well, now there was no escape. Those old ideas about cooking being for someone else would have to change. I had to face the future, for Jenny's sake and for my family's sake. If the food processor had defeated me, I would try to make it up against the microwave. If it was me against the kitchen, then it was up to me to adjust. Someday, my day would come. Someday.

(To be continued . . .)

Facing Our Fears

MAYBE WE WERE more anxious than we admitted about starting a family at our ages, but we were full of imagined fears while Joan was pregnant. Somehow, we couldn't believe someone as wonderful as Jenny could enter our lives.

No imagined fears prepared us for the day Joan fell. She was six months pregnant. She had gone from her office to the dealer's garage to pick up her car after some repairs, when she stepped onto a wet spot on the concrete floor. She hit the floor on her knees, then thrust her arms out to break the rest of her fall.

When she got home, she quietly said something had happened that afternoon.

"I fell," she said, tears literally falling from her face. I thought her heart was breaking.

After trying to comfort her, I called the obstetrician and got the answering service, since it was nearly 6:00 P.M. I said it was an emergency and described what had happened. The sympathetic operator said the doctor would call as soon as possible.

Joan lay on the couch and tried to relax. We strained to feel the faintest of movements from Jenny. Nothing. It was a long half-hour before the doctor called back. She listened to a description of the fall, and told us Jenny had certainly had a jolt but was probably all right because she was well protected in there. But we were to call if there were any problems, or if there was no movement at a time when Jenny usually was active.

We soon felt a few thumps from Jenny, and we began breathing again. Everything was safe and back to normal.

Facing a real fear might have pointed up the silliness of our imagined fears, but it didn't eliminate them. Before Jenny was born, we often found it hard to believe we actually would see her little face and hold her wrinkled, floppy little body. Would there someday be a little person coming down the stairs holding a teddy bear, saying "Mommy?" or "Daddy?" No, for some reason it didn't seem possible that it could happen for us.

Maybe we couldn't stand the thought of being happy, or were afraid of tempting fate by imagining it.

"I have a feeling like the feeling I had in the days before we got married," Joan said one night. "Before we got married I felt like it was something I wanted so much, I was afraid something would happen to prevent it—you would die, or I would die, and we would never get married. I have the same feeling now. Especially when I'm getting in the car. I feel like, 'OK, just let me make it home.' When I'm driving, I keep thinking, 'OK, now nobody hit me. Please, nobody hit me.'"

I knew what she meant. While I was still traveling in the final months of my old job, I kept thinking, "This airplane had better not go down because then Jenny won't have a father. And I'll never get to see her."

Some sort of fear must be built into us by culture. Joan said it was an Irish custom never to buy anything for a baby before it's born. She said her mother would never even buy a receiving blanket before any of her seven children were born. Only after the birth would she send out Dr. Vanderbeck for enough wrappings to get the baby home.

With Jenny due in December, Joan finally consented to let her friends and her mom give her a baby shower late in October. She wouldn't let herself feel eager until the last few days before the celebration.

Baby lore was new to me. But I had some creeping fears of my own, fears that those bad old days of too much alcohol and too little awareness would somehow make me unworthy of a little miracle like Jenny.

I had a talk with my friend John Madden—not the ex-coach and broadcaster, but a gifted clinical psychologist who had helped Joan and me through some hard times. He helped me through this one, too.

Sometimes a man can feel unworthy of joy or reward because of a case of guilt, or a feeling that he hasn't met some sort of standard. I had spent a lot of unsettled time building up those kinds of feelings. I needed to see there was nothing I had to do to be worthy of Jenny. She wasn't something I had to achieve.

It sounded silly, but an imaginative journey helped me clear things up, and I still take it sometimes. John had me envision climbing a mountain path to seek an answer to my questions from a wise old man. I couldn't avoid a mental picture of Mel Brooks' and Carl Reiner's comical "2,000-Year-Old Man," satirizing the search for the meaning of life.

I don't know why, but I bought into this imagined trip up the mountain, and I knew what the old man would say before we met. He didn't disappoint me. He said, simply: "This is a gift."

Maybe permission to feel worthy was all I wanted. I still needed to remind myself at times, but being Jenny's dad was all the achievement I ever needed.

"Hello, My Little Sweetheart!"

JENNY ROSE opened her left eye warily, just long enough to see that the light was too bright. Everything was so different now, especially the light.

Her perfect miniature hands were reaching into the air. I put the little finger of my left hand into her right hand, and she grasped it tightly. My daughter and I touched for the first time.

I had the nurse turn down the light in the warming tray. I bent closer and began talking to Jenny in a low soft voice.

"Hello, my beautiful little sweetheart," I said. "We've been waiting a long time to see you." She looked into my eyes, studying me. My daughter had seen me for the first time.

I will never forget Jenny's first moment of life on her own: 2:49 P.M., Wednesday, December 13, 1989. Jenny first felt the touch of the soft, strong hands of Dr. Ann Ressetar, as she opened her nostrils for her first breath and opened her mouth for her first cry after her startling journey through the birth canal. She was here to begin her new journey.

Joan and I had arrived at the hospital at 7:00 A.M. Our neighbor, Judy, Joan's close friend of long standing, drove us and stayed until we were settled. Joan was a week overdue, and coping with a difficult end to the pregnancy: she had been hospitalized twice with chest pains. We had decided to induce labor, before the decision could be made for us by another frightening episode. This was birth by appointment, we hoped.

By 8:30 A.M., Joan was receiving pitocin intravenously to induce labor. At about 10:00 A.M., the contractions began coming regularly, two to six minutes apart. The cervix had effaced, or thinned, enough for Dr. Ressetar to term it "mushy," but it still had not begun dilating to the needed ten centimeters. Despite the pitocin, we were preparing for a long siege.

But Joan's membranes (or "bag of waters," as they called it in our prenatal classes) broke at 11:20 A.M. Now there was no question: Jenny was coming today.

The pitocin was cranked up repeatedly. The contractions came fast and hard until they were starting about two minutes apart. They each lasted about a minute, so Joan had only a minute to recover between contractions: there was no time for the strategies from prenatal classes, except to make sure Joan kept breathing. I was squeezing her hand, talking to her, massaging her, helping her focus, helping her breathe through the contractions. Catherine, Joan's mom, and Kathy, Joan's sister, had joined us for support the rest of the way.

But when the contractions increased their burning intensity at around 1:00 P.M., Joan needed an epidural anesthetic to numb the lower half of her body. The anesthesiologist did a masterful job, explaining each step as he worked between contractions. When the epidural kicked in, Joan could still feel the contractions but she wasn't overwhelmed by them.

Still concerned about the lack of dilation, Dr. Ressetar was back at 2:00 P.M. for a pelvic examination. She reassured Joan about the anesthetic, then gasped.

"Oh, my gosh!" she said. "Joan, you're a full ten centimeters! We're going to have a baby here, right away! I have to scrub up now. When I get back, we have some work to do. It's time for you to start pushing."

When she returned, she gave Joan a quick course in pushing out the baby: deep breath, exhale, another deep breath, hold it in the middle of your chest, and push. I timed each push, counting out loud to ten. Joan pushed for about half an hour, at least three times per contraction. Then Dr. Ressetar stopped encouraging Joan long enough to motion me to the front.

"I want you to see something," she said, and there, just about to emerge, was milky-white scalp and dark matted hair—the top of Jenny's head. Time stopped for me.

But there was more pushing, at least one more contraction. I went back and began counting for Joan again. At eight, my voice broke. I swallowed and regained control. I wasn't ashamed of my emotions, but I needed to be strong for Joan and I didn't want to miss a second of what was happening.

Suddenly, Dr. Ressetar beckoned Kathy and Joan's mom to come closer. I could see they were entranced. I leaned forward. Dr. Ressetar reached out, and there was Jenny.

She held Jenny up for Joan to see. A nurse helped her clamp the umbilical cord, and she held out a scissors to me. "This is your job, Dad," Dr. Ressetar said. "Don't worry. She can't feel a thing."

My hand felt shaky, but I cut the surprisingly tough, rubbery cord between the two clamps. The nurse took Jenny to the warming tray, to monitor her temperature. I kissed Joan and we embraced, as Joan cried with pure joy. I felt tearful, but I also felt a surge of great prideful laughter.

Joan had more work to do, delivering the placenta. She sent me to Jenny's side. As I leaned over the warming tray, speaking to Jenny, my finger in her tight little fist with skin as soft as an aura, I heard Joan crying happily.

Our Jenny Rose was here.

The Hospital

The Chicago hospital where Jenny was born is one of the finest, but one rule applies to any hospital: try to leave as soon as you can. Even the best hospital, in the best circumstances, can make you crazy unless you are prepared to fight routine and bureaucracy to get what you want. We were prepared.

The hospital had carefully designed its "labor-delivery-recovery room." The medical apparatus was stashed in cabinets as unobtrusively as possible. The room was a "suite," with television, table, rocking chair, even a sofa and armchairs for guests and labor coaches, in addition to the Adel birthing bed. A stereo and tape deck provided music. But there was no closet. Clothes went into plastic bags.

The arrangements had been clear and thorough. We could have essentially whatever kind of birth experience we wanted. I could be at Joan's side all the time, with two additional "guests" for the birth. Joan could nurse Jenny soon after the birth. I could be in a private room with my wife and daughter both nights of our stay. We could have Jenny with us twenty-four hours a day if we wanted, and that's what we wanted.

But the hospital was part of the package, whether we wanted it or not.

Jenny was born at 2:49 P.M. on December 13. The shift changed at 11:00 P.M., when she was just over eight hours old, and routine required that Jenny be taken to the nursery to be weighed again, have her temperature monitored again, and be bathed. We OK'd the first two, but not the midnight bath. We couldn't see the sense of it, and we wouldn't part with Jenny that long. The next day, Joan received some invaluable help from the hospital's breastfeeding consultant. But the routine checks had begun again at 5:00 A.M. We became increasingly annoyed by routine, especially after waiting ninety minutes for some medication Joan had requested.

That night, I took charge. No one would get past me.

Around midnight, I heard a knock. I leapt from my cot and got to the door before the nurse could walk in. I was ready for a confrontation, bristling for a battle with the bureaucracy. I told the nurse my wife and daughter were sleeping. Could she please come back later?

"Oh, of course," she said reasonably, silently continuing down the corridor.

Victory. I closed the door and returned to the cot, feeling like a knight guarding the door to my ladies' chamber.

We held off much of the routine the final day, but there were two procedures we couldn't avoid. The pediatrician ordered a bilirubin blood test for jaundice. We were assured it was a routine procedure that would startle Jenny more than hurt her. I couldn't go into the nursery for the test, but I could watch through the window. I watched a technician stick Jenny's left heel and squeeze blood onto a slide. I watched the technician go to the phone on her desk. I watched my daughter crying and crying.

I pressed against the glass. I rapped on the door. I flagged down a nurse in the corridor, one who had been quite nice to us.

"Look at the way my baby is screaming!" I said, angry and near tears myself. "That's terrible, to leave her screaming like that!"

The nurse, probably familiar with paranoid first-time fathers, silently scurried back to the nurses' station to drop off her paperwork. She returned to the nursery, went to Jenny, and picked her up. We brought her back to the room together, as I tried to calm Jenny and myself. Newborn babies are not supposed to have tears yet, but tears were rolling down Jenny's left cheek.

Before Jenny could be discharged, she had to undergo a PKU (phenylketonuria) test, required by the State of Illinois for a rare but possibly serious bacterial disorder. After our experience with the jaundice test (negative), Joan had a long talk with our sympathetic nurse. Joan couldn't be in the nursery, but the nurse promised to hold Jenny and try to comfort her while Joan watched.

I wasn't there for this one. I had to go home, to shovel the snow from the front of our house and get our car ready for a new and precious passenger. Joan told me if I had seen the test, I would not have been able to stand it. Jenny's heel was stuck again, but this time she had to have enough blood squeezed out to cover six spots on a test card. Joan said as she watched Jenny crying, she could feel the pain of each squeeze.

These tests, of course, all make good medical sense. As upset as we were, I don't know how we would have reacted if something had actually been wrong with Jenny. But the hospital's apparent indifference to a baby's emotional well-being still disturbs me. Isn't birth a difficult and frightening enough experience, without adding to a baby's fears?

But we were almost done. I had the car out front. Next came the intricate discharging procedure, checking identifications with Joan to make sure Jenny was indeed our baby. The identity confirmed, Joan bundled up Jenny for the arctic cold. The nurse carried Jenny to the car and made sure she was placed in a child restraint seat (state law). We stuffed blankets around seven-pound Jenny to fit her into a seat designed for a child weighing up to forty pounds.

Finally, we slammed the car doors. I was taking my family home. The hospital would have to do without me.

New Parenthood

Coming Home

JENNY ROSE came home to a house with a Christmas tree, with lights glowing and presents already piling up around it. On the tape deck, Nat Cole sang "The Christmas Song."

Joan carried Jenny over to the "Moses basket" that was a present from Catherine, Jenny's grandmother, waiting there with a tearful smile. Joan unwrapped Jenny from her protection against that frigid December day and gently placed her in the basket. She turned to me for a long and full embrace. We both were in tears.

"I felt the same way every time I brought a child home," Catherine said.

Jenny was home. It still seemed unreal after all the waiting and imagining. We had pictured her many times lying safe and secure among the covers in that basket, and now she actually was here. Our house was different and our lives were different. We were a family now, in a family home.

Bringing Jenny home from the hospital took fifteen minutes of the best driving of my life. It had to be my best driving, because I had never been so nervous behind the wheel. Joan and Jenny were in the back, with Jenny strapped into her child restraint seat: I had a family depending on me to keep them safe. Driving had made me nervous while Joan was pregnant, but now I was a brake pedal away from panic. Every other car was a threat. But we made it home safely, and soon began making discoveries about Jenny and our life as a family.

We had anticipated needing help at the start, so Catherine came to stay with us for at least a week. We could not have known how much help we needed, or how valuable Catherine would be.

Catherine took over the house: breakfast, lunch, dinner, snacks and laundry. Catherine took Jenny for some extra love or a burp. Catherine took care of both of us, understanding everything. Catherine handled the constant deliveries of gifts and flowers.

Catherine went up and down the stairs before we even realized we needed something. But she made sure we both rested whenever we could, as we began the twenty-four-hour care needed by a newborn. She encouraged us when we were fumbly and unsure of ourselves. She was forbearing when we told her there were some things we would be doing differently than she had done with her own seven children. When Joan became sick one night and couldn't keep down her food, Catherine was there to comfort her and hold her head as tenderly as she ever had when Joan was a child.

Then, four days before Christmas, Catherine's older sister, Aunt Dos, flew in from New Jersey for the holidays. Aunt Dos, impishly energetic in her eighties, is a female Barry Fitzgerald-type character. She also was a career OB-GYN nurse in the Navy, rising to the rank of lieutenant commander in the reserves. She served in Navy hospitals from South Carolina to the South Pacific. When she advised, we listened, even if it meant enduring a meandering tale or two.

Our days and nights all revolved around Jenny, with all the confusion, fatigue, and frustration of learning to care for this new little person who needed us.

But at any moment, Jenny could make a face or a noise or a movement that transcended any other concern. We wondered at our good fortune in having this beautiful baby. We were surprised at her alertness, at her concentration on our faces as we talked to her or sang to her. We were happy and grateful for her calmness and patience with us, as we learned to change her, to dress her, to bathe her.

And there—wasn't that the beginning of a real smile? Baby authorities have always said those early smiles were the result of gas. But newer thought says they were "practice smiles," to begin Jenny's growth as a social person, as she learned to interact with us. She might well have been imitating all the smiles we gave her, and she actually seemed to imitate other facial movements at times: sticking out her tongue, or rounding her mouth into an "O."

Always, there was the closeness of Jenny, the new softness of her skin, the pure sweetness of her smell, the feel of her downy head against my cheek while I held her. And the sense of her complete and unconditional trust as she fell asleep in my arms.

Catherine took Aunt Dos home to prepare Christmas dinner. Christmas came and went before we knew it, with Jenny braving the journey to Catherine's house to meet some new relatives, and bearing up better than Mom and Dad.

That is, she bore up better after crying through much of the drive to Grandma's. She fell asleep just before we arrived, slept through the elevator ride up to Grandma's condo, slept through the undressing and placement into a bassinet. We were relieved that she slept, though one guest was disappointed after having lifted a few toasts awaiting our arrival. "Aw, let's wake her up so we can see her," this guest said.

"Touch her and I'll smack you," I said, without thinking. Fortunately, I said it under my breath. Only Joan's younger sister heard me, sitting next to me at the table. She had to cough into her napkin to hide her laughter. I picked up my own napkin and we coughed side by side. Nobody woke up Jenny.

Somehow, we had blinked: if this was Christmas, then Jenny was almost two weeks old. We had experienced minutes that went by like hours, especially at night, but we also had days that felt like seconds. This irreplaceable, exhausting time already was passing too quickly.

Burned-out Parents

AT FOUR WEEKS, Jenny was a thriving, beautiful, nine-pound baby with two deranged zombies for parents.

We were desperate for sleep. One night, I was sure I had the answer.

"Jenny, I have a deal for you," I said. "If you fall asleep in the next five minutes, I'll buy you a pony."

She looked interested, but ultimately rejected a deal she is certain to regret some day.

All the baby books say: "You won't get much sleep the first few months." But nothing prepared us for the depth of our fatigue, or the draining of our emotions. No one told me there would be a night when I almost lost control.

Jenny was having her first growth spurt, starting at ten days. Joan was breastfeeding continually, but poor Jenny was miserable most of the time. She slept fitfully, and we slept hardly at all.

On the third night, Joan desperately needed to soak in the tub, to relieve the soreness in the sutures from her episiotomy. Jenny had been crying intermittently for hours. But she had just been fed and I was sure I could handle her alone.

All I accomplished was to make her cry more loudly, more forlornly, more piercingly. My daughter was screaming, as if begging me for help, and I couldn't help her. My head ached. My heart ached.

I began tightening up, until I was on the verge of yelling at Jenny to stop crying, to stop making me nuts. I made do with a shouted whisper, directed up toward the ceiling: "I can't stand this!" Somehow I had the presence of mind to set Jenny down on her changing table, keeping her steady with my hand on her chest. I tried to steady myself by breathing deeply.

Joan came out of the bath, hugged me, and told me to go to another room and close the door. She would take over. Jenny had been crying in my arms for twenty minutes that felt like twenty hours.

In those helpless twenty minutes, I saw the line between control and lack of control, between doing all I reasonably could and doing something stupid. I saw the anger produced by my own frustration and helplessness, and it was frightening. Could I have done something abusive? I was shaken by the thought.

The next night at 3:00 A.M., when Joan reached the snapping point and said, "I have to get away," I understood. This time, I was able to stay calm long enough to help soothe Jenny and give Joan a break.

"This is the hardest thing I've ever done," Joan said. "I didn't think it could be harder than that last month of pregnancy. That had its own hard parts. But this is harder."

Fatigue was bad enough. Combined with helplessness and frustration, it pushed us to some of our darkest points. We wondered if we also had a physical disadvantage in being older parents, in lacking the stamina of our younger days. At forty, I couldn't do some of the things I did routinely at twenty-five or thirty—including getting along on little sleep.

Joan's hardships were compounded by her recovery from pregnancy and birth, and by the physical and emotional demands of breastfeeding, before even considering the "forties factor." Joan's mom was twenty-eight when Joan was born; my mom was twenty-three when I was born. That difference was sure to count in the first weeks, when Jenny needed to be fed every hour or so during the day and woke up about every two hours at night.

Tired and helpless, we began asking ourselves those two dreaded questions: "What are we doing wrong?" and "Does Jenny have colic?"

Our love and care didn't seem to be enough. We were unsure of ourselves. We didn't know what Jenny needed: sleep? stimulation? closeness? change of scenery? change of position? change of diaper? music? rocking? bouncing? Anything that worked once never seemed to work twice. We felt badly about the way we were handling things, and the worse we felt, the worse we slept.

We got two pieces of advice from our pediatrician. First, Jenny might have a little touch of colic. That's the baby doctor's equivalent of "stomach flu." It's something to say when no one really knows what's wrong. Second, the best ways to handle Jenny's crying were to hold her as calmly and closely as possible, trying not to add to her miseries by switching positions every minute, and trying to distance ourselves from her distress.

In other words, while Jenny was crying in our arms, we had to tell ourselves she wasn't crying because we were bad parents. Crying was her only means of communication, the only way she could tell us how lousy she felt. When I felt exasperated, or began to feel angry, the problem was within myself. I had to grapple with my own feelings of helplessness and inadequacy—worsened by fatigue. I had to tell myself I was doing the best I could, and that being calm and loving was more help to Jenny than I realized.

It was a hard lesson to live in that difficult early time. Looking back, it was the hardest lesson of all.

High-Need Baby

DID JENNY INHERIT JOAN'S PERSONALITY? She wanted it all, right now, including dessert.

It was hard to keep up with Jenny's needs, harder still to anticipate them successfully. And when she cried, there were times when that was her greatest need: simply to cry, as hard as she could, for as long as she needed, to get through her difficulties.

Traditionally, Jenny would be called a "colicky" or "fussy" baby. But "colicky" made her sound as if she was vaguely unhealthy, spewing out sour milk. "Fussy" made her sound like my second-grade teacher back in Brooklyn, who wore steel-rimmed glasses, high collars and sensible shoes, and always seemed to be sniffing at some faint, unpleasant odor.

We preferred to think of Jenny as a "high-need" baby.

Jenny was a baby of extremes, of soaring highs and plummeting lows. She could be intensely absorbed in viewing everything around her. She could be entranced in her crib, watching her mobile and listening to her music box; smiling, cooing, and gurgling, as close as could be to talking; waving her arms and legs with glee. Her face could absolutely glow with a smile that showed happiness clear down to her soul. She also could cry inconsolably, for hours on end, impervious to any attempt to calm her or lift her spirits. If her delight seemed limitless, so did her sorrow.

In her first few weeks, it seemed as if Jenny's crying might have a physiological source, like gastric distress. She was not easy to burp after feeding. She seemed to be struggling to get food passed through her system. She was a gulper at the breast, likely to take in air with her milk, and seldom nursed more than seven or eight minutes at a time.

But as we got to know Jenny, gastric distress was simply too simple and limited an answer for what was troubling her. And it didn't go away.

I remembered Jenny's first hours in the hospital, the way she seemed to be seeing and hearing everything that happened, looking into every corner of the room. Catherine had said, "She's so alert!"

Even one of the nurses had commented on how "observant" Jenny was.

I began to form my own theory, and I became more convinced of it with time: Jenny's personality was just too complex for her to handle. She was too alert, too curious, too aware of her environment, beyond her body's ability to provide the means to stimulate or comfort herself at her early stage of development. She was like a real little person in a baby's body. Her primary problem wasn't gas, but frustration.

The big, encyclopedic baby reference books are of little use for a baby like Jenny. They are too lofty and detached, trying to aim at some mythical "average" child. A baby who doesn't fit their neat categories can seem to be an aberration. When you read one of those big books and nothing seems to apply to your baby, you can feel pretty isolated.

That's how we began to feel, and we became "high-need" parents. We needed wisdom from somewhere. We needed some confirmation of our experience, and when we looked hard enough, we found it.

We found it from other parents who had hard times with similar babies. I don't know how we would have gotten through the first few weeks, for example, without the help and sympathy of Joan's younger sister, Kathy, whose daughter had been a high-need baby. I know we could not have survived without the help and comfort provided by Joan's mom. And we found a source book that seemed to be written by a real person who had experienced real babies, who cried long and loud enough to leave their parents shaken.

The Fussy Baby: How to Bring Out the Best in Your High-Need Child, by Dr. William Sears, was a revelation. We saw that we weren't crazy, we weren't alone, and (thank heavens) we weren't doing everything wrong. Sears even mirrored our own thinking on the first page: "The term 'fussy baby' is a bit unfair . . . I prefer to call this special type of baby the 'high-need baby.' This is not only a kinder term, but it more accurately describes why these babies act the way they do and what level of parenting they need."

Sears' profile of a "high-need baby" was remarkably close to Jenny. She was supersensitive to her environment and often easily disturbed. She was intense and demanding. She needed physical contact, but she often protested and stiffened when she was held. She wasn't satisfied easily or consistently, and what worked once in calming her didn't usually work twice.

Our challenge was to be highly responsive parents, but Sears held out a promise for the outcome: "The intense baby may become the creative child; the sensitive infant, the compassionate child. The little 'taker' may later become a big giver." It's likely, then, that Jenny also inherited Joan's depth of compassion and her limitless capacity for giving.

We began to understand Jenny, a major step in our ability to cope with her needs. We had to give her our best, so she could bring out the best in herself.

Learning to Cope

IF JENNY COULD HAVE LISTED her favorite places in her little world during those hard times, one of them would have been my left shoulder.

She went to sleep on my left shoulder most nights in those early months. It was one of the few places where she was sure to calm down, though how long it took was an open question. One night when she was about two months old, I held her constantly, except for feedings and changings, from 6:00 P.M. until 1:00 A.M., when she finally slipped off to sleep after her exhausting, tear-filled struggle.

If there was something special about my left shoulder, sometimes there was also something special about the top of the clothes dryer, with its combination of heat, noise and vibration, while Joan and I played with Jenny or tried to soothe her. A high-need baby requires highly resourceful parents.

Joan and I had decided before Jenny was born that we would be "full-contact" parents. It was in our nature to be that deeply involved, but our thinking was crystallized during Joan's pregnancy by reading Ashley Montagu's *Touching: The Human Significance of the Skin*. A baby, Montagu says, gets most of her information about her new world through her skin, the one sensory organ that is fully mature at birth. We decided we would hold Jenny as much as she needed and pick her up whenever she began to cry, never letting her "cry it out" alone in her crib. We never imagined how much contact this actually would involve—or how many people would admonish us for "spoiling" Jenny.

Her intense needs left us shaken and worn out. Joan was so exhausted, after her difficult pregnancy, that she seemed near collapse. We weren't just giving rise to groundless fears; that was her doctor's diagnosis.

We got as much help as we could, but it was sleep that we needed most. At about five weeks, Jenny began sleeping five to five-and-a-half hours at night instead of waking every few hours to nurse. She gradually built up her night's sleep to between six and seven hours by her tenth week. It took another week or so before Joan and I stopped waking at 3:00 A.M. from habit. We hoped the change was permanent; it wasn't, but we did receive a few weeks' reprieve.

New parents can be devastated by sleep deprivation, with its double threat of anxiety and fatigue. Saying "sleep when the baby sleeps" is good advice, but it assumes you don't have to do anything about meals, laundry, or bills—and it also assumes a baby who naps at some length, with some predictability.

Sleeping at night, even temporarily, made a dramatic difference in our ability to cope, because Jenny seemed to need a lot of everything except sleep. She was awake most of the day. Those times when she was wonderfully alert and playful could disintegrate quickly into pain and tears. She needed to be held to relax enough for sleep. Always sensitive to her surroundings, she would wake up quickly if we tried to set her down before she was sleeping soundly. We devised the "limp arm" test: Jenny was not ready to be set down until her arm could be lifted without resistance, and drop of its own weight when let go. Fortunately for us, our stretch of improved sleep kept us from being pushed over the edge.

Sleep helped our stamina, and Dr. Sears continued to give us direction. He confirmed our "hands-on" or "full-contact" approach, which he called "attachment parenting." He confirmed my feelings about Jenny's hypersensitivity to her environment: a baby like Jenny had what he called an "immature shut-down reflex," so she could not easily retreat into sleep when she was overwhelmed by stimulus, as most babies could.

Sears also advised trying to anticipate Jenny's needs, alleviating some of her need to cry and helping her learn to cry more "effectively": this meant helping her learn that she didn't always have to cry to have her needs met. We continued to hold Jenny much of the time, often "wearing" her in a sling or front pouch, though nothing was as satisfying as our arms.

We were doing everything we could for Jenny, but what about ourselves? We still had to cope with her crying and with our own frayed emotions. Sears advised regarding a high-need baby as someone who needs comforting, not someone with a disease. He also pointed out that we are more likely to be sympathetic to someone with an obvious physical cause for his pain; otherwise, we are likely to become suspicious and feel we are being manipulated.

The answer, for me, came again from my psychologist friend John. He and his wife had adopted a five-month-old boy who had been born prematurely, then spent his first two months in a hospital and his next three months in foster homes.

To handle the exceptionally high needs of his son, John envisioned "counseling" him. When his son was crying and thrashing in his arms, John took it as a sign that his son felt safe and secure enough with him to express his pain and anguish. John admitted he couldn't always make it all the way through these "counseling sessions," but he made it through many. When the crying was at its worst, John envisioned himself giving "heroic" counseling.

So when Jenny was crying, I tried to be her hero. Instead of saying or thinking, "What is wrong with you?" I tried to say: "Tell Dad what's wrong," or "I know it's bad," or "Tell Dad how it hurts." It was difficult, but it worked for both of us—when I had the presence of mind to try it. Often, I didn't understand what she was trying to tell me, but I tried hard to learn.

I hoped Jenny understood me. And I hoped she would always feel she could find safety and comfort on my left shoulder.

The Rewards

AT TWO MONTHS, Jenny was still far from saying, "I love you, Daddy," or "I love you, Mommy." She couldn't laugh, or jump into our arms for a hug. She didn't understand our words when we said we loved her, though we hoped the meaning was getting through.

At two months, we were still experiencing those times when other parents said, "It gets better," telling us the rewards were yet to come. But when I took stock—amid all the hardships—the rewards were grand.

They began each morning, when we awakened. Our first sight was of Jenny, and hers were of Joan and me. The first time we picked up Jenny and held her each day, we would breathe in the pure fragrance of her skin. No day of my life had ever begun more perfectly.

And Jenny's smile: to see one was to be lifted from your feet. One smile could cancel the memory of any sleepless night.

Jenny began smiling when she was about a week old, little shadows of smiles when our faces were near. They appeared and faded quickly until she was twenty-two days old. That night, Joan and I were talking to her and playing with her. Jenny was in Joan's arms, looking around, listening to both of us. She focused on me, and she seemed to be concentrating, as if to say, "Hey, I think I know you."

Then her whole face was filled with a smile: her mouth in a wide-open grin, her nose wrinkled, her eyes crinkled almost shut. She waved her arms and kicked her feet. It was a smile such as I had never seen. It was Jenny's first real smile of delight, and I was there to see it.

That smile was among my greatest rewards. But I was also rewarded simply by being around for whatever happened, from moment to moment, whether in happy times or hard times.

By giving up my sportswriting job to stay home and write and be with Jenny, by sharing her care fully with Joan in those first months, I gained a priceless opportunity. I was able to witness the start of my daughter's life almost minute by minute. I was able to share all the wonders and difficulties to a degree most men are unable to know. I was as close as possible to my daughter, physically and emotionally, from the moment Joan gave birth to her.

What greater reward could there have been than seeing Jenny emerge from the womb? That night, I took Jenny into my arms for the first time. I had helped to create this life, and now I could sense the warmth of her breath on my cheek, and feel her racing heartbeat. I rocked her to sleep in my arms, and I don't think I ever could experience a more complete and unconditional trust.

In two months, Jenny gave me a new understanding of myself. The first sign of change came during the first time I held her. I had never been especially fond of other people's babies, never had a desire to hold and cuddle them. Like most men, I was skittish about holding such new, fragile, and mysterious creatures.

But not with Jenny. I held Jenny with nothing but love and confidence. My arms and hands were gentle, calm, and strong, and I hope I communicated that sense of myself to Jenny in our first contact. Joan says she knows I did. I hope Jenny will always feel those qualities coming from me. I found those new depths by becoming her dad, so I owe them to her.

But the rewards didn't have to be so complex, or require such introspection. For instance, I loved to see the bond between Joan and Jenny, the closeness of mother and daughter, whether Joan was giving Jenny a bath or singing her a lullaby. And what could compare to Jenny's happiness as she lay kicking and smiling and waving her hands, mesmerized by the mobile hanging at the side of her crib? Perhaps the sight was matched only by Jenny sleeping peacefully, living in dreams we could not know. Sometimes Joan and I would actually delay our own much-needed sleep to watch Jenny asleep, carried away by her beauty.

I was tickled by the "conversations" Jenny had with Joan and me. We talked to her and she replied with her growing vocabulary of sounds, from "Hi" and "Aaahh" to several others that resisted description. She kept surprising us with new sounds.

And some of my favorite memories will be of the times Jenny curled up into an almost fetal position against my shoulder, her hands tucked under her chin, her knees tucked up under her tummy. Her feet and her little bottom fit into one of my hands. We called her "Jenny-ball" in that configuration.

Whatever the difficulties in caring for Jenny's constant needs at that early age, whether handling her colicky crying or changing her diapers, I didn't feel wanting for rewards. But maybe I'm just an easy guy to please. Jenny probably will find she has a real pushover for a dad.

Dealing with People

THE NIGHT AFTER JENNY WAS BORN, she cried and cried until I rocked her to sleep in my arms in our hospital room. She finally slept peacefully, and I was a proud father.

Then I told someone what I had done.

"Oh, no! That's a bad start," I was told. "You shouldn't rock her to sleep like that. You'll spoil her."

"You may be right," I said, thinking quickly. "But I think I can break her of the habit by the time she's eighteen or so."

I had discovered the flip side of people's extraordinary generosity toward babies: people also are extraordinarily generous with advice, whether you want to hear it or not. People seem to think babies are in the public domain. They will touch them, grab them, poke noses in their faces, attempt to pick them up without asking permission, and commit intrusions they would not dare with an adult. They don't seem to realize how severely they are testing the parents' restraint.

Most often, people want to tell you that you aren't doing something the "right way." And they love to warn that you are "spoiling" your baby.

We were easy targets, the way we picked Jenny up whenever she cried, sometimes carrying her for hours. We fed her when she was hungry, instead of according to an arbitrary schedule. Joan continued to nurse her, instead of giving her formula or cereal at three months. We were easy targets for people ready to admonish us that we were spoiling Jenny.

Were we spoiling Jenny? Not as far as we were concerned—not by attending to her needs and trying to make her feel as secure and loved as possible. Our trusted guide, Dr. William Sears, said that not answering a baby's cries was far more likely to produce a clingy, whiny, and spoiled child. In *The Fussy Baby*, Sears wrote: "A baby whose cries have been promptly responded to early on learns to trust and to anticipate that a response will be forthcoming." He cited two studies at Johns Hopkins University, demonstrating "that children whose mothers had responded promptly to their cries as infants were less likely to use crying as a means of communication at one year of age." In *Becoming a Father*, he wrote that spoiling "describes something put on a shelf and left to rot. Babies do not get spoiled by being held. Babies spoil if they are not held."

I was sure I hadn't spoiled Jenny by rocking her to sleep her troubled first night. By her eleventh week, she was falling asleep most nights after nursing at around 11:00 P.M. Occasionally, she did need to be rocked. But if I had spoiled her, she would have demanded more rocking, not less.

Why do people insist on giving baby advice? One reason certainly is the desire to be helpful. But another may be what I began to call "Lone Ranger Syndrome": wanting to ride in on a white horse, establish law and order, and gallop off into the sunset, leaving behind a host of admirers who can't give enough thanks to that masked man. The Lone Ranger can be today's hero without facing tomorrow's problems.

There may be more complicated reasons for advice without consent. People may need to reconfirm their own child-raising methods as being the "right" ones. They may need to assuage their own doubts about what they did. They may want others to endure what they endured. They may want to correct errors they remember from their own childhoods.

Whatever their reasons, I was never sure how to deflect their unwanted advice. The best way was probably to say something noncommittal, like: "Thank you for the advice. I will consider it." Unfortunately, I usually forgot to say this. But mostly, I tried simply to ignore the advice and avoid ill feeling, because I also began to learn about the generosity, concern, and care that people can extend to a baby and to new parents.

Generosity toward Jenny and toward us was not confined to material gifts. Friendships can become closer when someone calls to ask "How are you doing?" and listens sympathetically when you need to talk. The best friends would ask, "What can we do? How can we help?" Bringing over a pot of homemade soup for dinner can cement an enduring loyalty.

You expect empathy from good friends, but other people may surprise you. I had reached the limit with one woman who repeatedly told me how much I was spoiling Jenny, but then she stopped and smiled.

"My daughters are twenty-eight and thirty years old," she said. "But I still feel like they're my babies. Can you believe that?"

Yes, I believed her. Just as I believed an often-sardonic executive and salesman who has a hard time hiding his love for his own children, and who gave us this message when Jenny was about a month old. It was worth enduring all that other advice.

"You're about to begin a wonderful time," he said. "You're about to re-experience your entire life, through your child's eyes."

Three Months

When Jenny reached the age of three months, we were told, there would be a dramatic change.

And there was: She threw up.

She had never thrown up before. Her usual milk overflow was a dribble from the corner of her lips. I was startled and frightened when I saw milk gushing from her mouth, cascading onto and over my shoulder. It seemed like more milk than she could possibly have contained.

A dramatic change in behavior is one of the reasons to call your pediatrician. I called our pediatrician. After asking about color (milky white) and the presence of blood (none), and hearing me say several times that she never had thrown up before, he gave his verdict.

"Babies throw up sometimes," he said. "She's only twelve weeks old. She'll be going through a lot of changes."

Mostly, she was the same Jenny: as alert and sensitive as ever, capable of great emotional demonstrations, from joy to anguish. She didn't sleep much during the day, she was still wakeful at night, and she needed plenty of holding and stimulus to fill her time. But as her mind and body grew, she developed new ways to amuse and comfort herself, and new ways to make contact with her ever-expanding world.

One of the most welcome changes for Jenny was the weather. During some unseasonably summery days in mid-March, we were able to get her into the car and take her out for walks without stuffing her into a snowsuit and hat and bundling her in a blanket.

Jenny was transformed. She used to wail from the instant we began lowering her into her snowsuit, and continued through the installation into the car seat and most of the car ride. But dressed simply in a one-piece coverall, free to look all around herself and with her arms and legs unencumbered, she saw the ride as a fascinating experience instead of an ordeal. On the way up Lake Shore Drive from Chicago to Evanston, Jenny looked intently out the side and back windows and watched the trees and scenery roll by. What a treat.

She loved being outdoors the rest of the afternoon, even when caught in the rain during a walk with Joan. She picked up her head and inspected everything around her. She held onto the thin branch of a small tree. She raised up and braced herself against the wind, like the prow of a ship meeting a wave. Her world was growing.

Her interior world was also expanding. She had been experimenting with her hands for several weeks. She had discovered that sucking furiously on her fingers and fist was a terrific pastime, and could help her comfort herself in times of distress. She made increasing contact with her own body, beginning with looking at her hands an inch in front of her eyes. She played with her hands together in front of her face. She began reaching down to touch her abdomen, her legs, her ankles. She began to take notice of her feet, holding them up for inspection and moving her toes around.

She began intentionally touching things around her in her crib, reaching out to her soft, fuzzy "cow jumping over the moon" music box and several of her stuffed animals. She even turned toward the music box and whimpered until I wound it up to produce the music. She loved it when I shook a pair of rattles near her face, and would hold them briefly if I placed them in her hands. She grabbed her blanket in her fist and brought it to her mouth. Lying on her back on the floor, she even began kicking at the figures hanging above her from her "Muppet" swing set.

Her sense of play grew, and she could be amused in her crib (with help from Mom and Dad) for as long as forty-five minutes. Her "vocabulary" expanded. At times she would lie in the crib and "talk" to her overhanging black-and-white mobile (especially the drawing of a face) for a quarter of an hour. Sometimes she seemed to be describing her entire range of emotions, cooing and babbling through smiles and sadness. Her face would scrunch up; she would be on the verge of tears, but she kept right on talking until she got to the next episode. And she loved having Joan read her poems by A. A. Milne each morning after her "breakfast."

One day, playing with Joan brought out the happiest change of all: Jenny laughed. Joan was nuzzling her and kissing her tummy, and the laugh was unmistakable. She had loved having her tummy kissed for a few weeks by that point, wiggling and breaking into a wide, round smile. Now there were laughing sounds, two and three little squeaks in a row.

We had this new, delightful reward: we could make our daughter laugh. As Jenny grew, our joy grew with her.

The Battle of the Bottle

Jenny looked up at me with suspicion and hurt in her eyes, along with her tears.

"What are you trying to do to me?" she seemed to be saying.

What I was trying to do was give her breast milk in a bottle, which she would not take. In fact, she took a swing at the bottle, knocked it out of my hand, and sent it flying out of the crib.

Jenny and I were beginning the adjustment to a new way of life, with her mom not around all the time.

Joan returned to work early in March of 1990, just before Jenny was twelve weeks old. More accurately, Joan was returning to a regular schedule of being in her office. As the president of her company, she had been working throughout her maternity leave. Several business meetings had been held in our home, the fax machine was continually whirring out memos and documents, and many of Joan's hoped-for nap times had turned into long sessions on the telephone.

But it was time for Joan to go back to the office, every morning. She could create a flexible schedule, and our home is about ten minutes away from her office. She could come home for lunch and continue to nurse Jenny. She could ease into the afternoons by working the telephone from home, or continuing to hold meetings in our dining room. So Joan would not have to leave for an entire day, and I would be around all the time. We did not have to depend on a babysitter, and we did not have to face the decision of whether to place Jenny in daycare. We thought we had an ideal setup for the transition.

But as soon as Joan walked out the door that first morning, Jenny knew something had changed.

Jenny knew that Joan was not as available as she had been, and that she was suddenly down to one parent instead of two for hours at a time. She was upset and irritable for much of the morning during the first two weeks Joan was at work. She needed a lot of holding. And when I offered her the bottle, she cried, got angry, and pushed it away. Her anger grew until she threw that haymaker.

But the bottle seemed almost a secondary issue. The real issue was apparent when Joan came home and Jenny couldn't get to her quickly enough. Jenny missed her mom.

"I think I feel worse about that than I do about her having to take a bottle," Joan said. "An occasional bottle of breast milk doesn't seem so bad compared to her having to adjust to being separated from her mother this early. And I know how lucky we are. I know there are people who have a far worse situation than we have, and mothers who have had to leave their babies after a matter of weeks."

Even when parents are able to stay with their baby for as long as six months, the separation finally imposed by economic reality can be difficult, if not traumatic. We knew a family where the two working parents were able to arrange consecutive leaves to care for their daughter. Mom was at home with her the first three months before returning to work, and Dad stayed home (although without pay) the next three months. Then they had to place their daughter in daycare at the age of six months. They live in a nice suburb, and they found a good daycare center. But it was difficult for parents and child. Dad remembers the day when his daughter cried long and hard and clung to his jacket when he attempted to leave her at the daycare center.

A story like that one made our hearts ache, while it also made us feel fortunate again that we didn't need to find daycare for Jenny. But we still had to get through the day, and the struggle over the bottle could make the day very long.

Our strategy was to offer the bottle to Jenny once each day, for no more than five or six minutes—if even that long. On the third trial, Jenny drained the half-ounce of breast milk. She had protested strongly and wouldn't accept the bottle, but soon calmed down for a five-minute nap. Borrowing from tactics Joan had used during difficult nursing times, I eased the bottle into Jenny's mouth as soon as she awoke. But it was the only time she accepted the bottle. She literally punched it away from her face on one attempt, and another time she knocked it across the crib. She was not happy.

Neither was I. My determination to feed Jenny could lead me to overrun the time limit and try to force just one more attempt, producing anger in both of us. After one disastrous "extra effort," I flung the bottle across the room myself.

I saw no reason why Jenny should not take the bottle; it was the same breast milk she had been taking all along. Jenny saw no reason why she should accept this poor substitute for Joan, and when I was honest about it, I really could not blame her. We were at an impasse. Somewhere there had to be a solution.

All I had to do was find it.

*Options:
Daycare and the
Daddy Track*

Daycare Directions and Questions

From her first breath, Jenny got all our attention. We didn't want her to be out of sight, out of hearing, out of touch.

We knew how lucky we were to be home with Jenny as much as we were, with one parent home all the time. We felt that making her the center of our attention, through her first year and beyond, was the best choice for her care and development.

And we had the luxury of making that choice. We had the luxury of not facing a day of separation when Jenny was three months old, or six months old, a day when both Joan and I had to leave the house for work in the morning, leaving Jenny behind or taking her to a daycare center. Maybe we had just waited too long to have a child to be willing to miss a minute of contact.

When we got through Jenny's first year, we always felt fortunate that we hadn't had to rely on daycare. We were concerned about the effect a group setting might have had on a high-need (or "colicky") baby like Jenny. In a daycare center, would an overworked caregiver have had the time or the emotional capacity to offer Jenny the constant holding and comforting that she needed—and that we were able to give her? It just would not have worked for us, or for her.

But we also knew we were going against the trend. And for many families, either with single parents or two working parents, there is no alternative to daycare.

On any given day, at least 6 million American preschool children are being cared for outside their homes. Look at it another way: if all these children were in one giant daycare center, there would be more mouths to feed at snack time than in the entire state of Massachusetts.

Daycare center enrollment quadrupled from 1976 to 1990, to a level of some 5 million children, according to the National Child Care Survey released November 6, 1991 (reported in the Washington *Post*). The study said there were more than 80,000 centers that had room for 5.3 million children and were operating at 90 percent capacity; another 118,000 regulated family daycare homes could handle an additional 860,000 children. And those are just the regulated, "official" venues. Those statistics can't take into account more informal arrangements.

Adding to the growth, companies like Stride-Rite, DuPont, and Sears have been in the forefront of businesses offering on-site daycare for their employees. Marriott has begun providing daycare centers for its employees at some hotels. IBM is in the midst of a five-year, $25-million program to provide child-care centers and care programs for the elderly.

Study after study has shown that it's good business for companies to pay attention to their employees' child-care concerns; companies with family-oriented attitudes and benefits show higher productivity and less absenteeism, enjoy more loyalty among employees, and gain a valuable edge in attracting new workers.

But there are persistent questions about daycare in general and early daycare in particular. Penelope Leach nearly fomented a rebellion with an interview in *Parenting* magazine in July 1991.

"For infants, that vital, continuous one-on-one attention just cannot be achieved in a daycare center's group settings," said Leach, whose *Your Baby and Child* has sold more than 2 million copies in the United States and has been translated into twenty-eight languages.

In later interviews, Leach stressed that she thought daycare could be valuable for toddlers at the age of two or three, who could learn valuable lessons in social skills while dealing with other children and adults in group situations. But she was adamant about the best situation for the first year or two of a child's life: at home, with a parent, preferably the mother, or in a stable, homelike situation with one primary caregiver. In an interview with the *Christian Science Monitor*, she said current research shows "that if a baby doesn't get securely attached to his mother or to whomever is caring for him during the day, he may end up being the child in kindergarten who has had independence forced upon him, and who doesn't listen to adults, who is disruptive and who is hard to teach."

Much of the debate on daycare focuses on "quality." The National Child Care Survey showed that costs basically held steady from 1976 to 1990. But for the overall cost to hold steady that long, other costs had to drop—and the drops came in areas directly affecting quality. Pay for caregivers dropped 25 percent, to $11,000; the child-to-staff ratio went up (25 percent), as did group size (16 percent).

Centers that care for infants and toddlers, the very places where "quality" is most important, showed the biggest changes in the wrong direction. Among centers caring for one-year-old children, the average group size rose to ten and the average child-staff ratio rose to nearly seven to one. Both numbers were near the limits recommended by most child-care experts. And there was a high turnover in caregivers, about 40 percent annually in private facilities when government programs were separated out.

Every finding seems to raise another question.

A study of eight-year-olds in Sweden showed that children who entered daycare before their first birthday performed better on achievement tests and seemed less anxious and more persistent than children who began at a later age. But a similar study of eight-year-olds in Texas found that those in daycare since infancy had poor grades and test scores, and were judged by parents and teachers to have poor relationships with friends and were difficult to discipline.

The major difference: Swedish daycare is highly regulated and subsidized; Texas daycare has minimal regulation.

And yet another study is coming: in mid-1990, the National Study of Young Children's Lives launched a five-year study of 1,200 infants, including a comparison of the developmental effects of working mothers who return to work during their child's first year and mothers who stay home with their children. The study will follow the families during the children's first thirty-six months. It looms as the first definitive attempt to compare home care with daycare. But given the increasing financial pressures on the American family in the last two decades, no study has yet come up with an answer to the key daycare question: what would many families do without it?

Lucky

WHEN I QUIT MY JOB to stay home with Jenny, we knew we faced some family belt-tightening. Losing my paycheck meant our income would drop by more than one-third. But it was our choice, and we knew we could afford it.

All across America, families faced a similar cut in income during the years 1973 to 1990. But it wasn't their choice, and they couldn't afford it.

We read the news on April 15, 1992: "Young families with children have significantly less money than their counterparts did a generation ago and suffer from child poverty rates that are twice as high, the Children's Defense Fund said in a study issued today. Incomes in those families have dropped by 32 percent, the study found, and the child poverty rate is now a sobering 40 percent." (*New York Times*)

Young families with children were defined as those families headed by a parent under thirty years of age; about half of all American children are born into that kind of family. In 1973, a young family's income was $27,765; but in 1990, a young family had to get along on $18,844 (the figures are held constant for inflation and expressed in 1990 dollars).

Imposing numbers, but what do they mean?

Let's say you were a "pre-baby-boomer," born in 1945 and anticipating the trend. You grew up in the postwar prosperity of the 1950s, and by 1973, at twenty-eight, you were an average American with a family, with an average American's income of nearly $28,000. You were comfortable, and content with the anticipation that your child would do even better than you'd done.

Cut to 1990. Your child is twenty-five with a new average American family, trying to get along on the new average income—less than $19,000. That one-third drop in income means your child has one-third less money to buy food and clothing for your grandchild; one-third less money for rent or a mortgage; one-third less money for doctors and dentists; one-third less money for Christmas presents.

These figures were compiled by the Children's Defense Fund and the Northeastern University Center for Labor Market Studies, analyzing data from the Census Bureau's Current Population Survey, an annual sample of about 60,000 households. And the numbers showed that the people who could least afford to have their incomes slashed were the hardest hit.

Suppose your child had quit high school, gone right to work, and soon started a family. By 1990, his or her average income was only $10,213—a 46 percent drop from where you had been at a similar time in your life.

Suppose your daughter had grown up to be a single parent. In 1990, the average income for a young family headed by a single female was a dismal $7,256. And in 1990, 37 percent of young families were single-parent families.

And what of the children? What happened to them as family income deteriorated? The saddest consequence became apparent in another CDF study released July 7, 1992: The number of American children living in poverty increased by more than 1 million in the 1980s to a total of 11 million children, with the poverty rates rising in thirty-three states.

Nearly one child in five (18 percent) lived in families below the federal poverty line in 1989. That included 39.8 percent of all black children and 38.8 percent of American Indian children; 32.2 percent of Hispanic children; 17.1 percent of Asian-American children; and 12.5 percent of white children.

Let's look at an average schoolroom in 1990. If there are thirty children in the class, five might come from impoverished families. Those five children might be hungry every day. They might not have a decent place to sleep at night. They might not be able to see a doctor when they're sick. And if the thirty children in that class are black, you can more than double the numbers: that means eleven or twelve children of deprivation. Children's advocates see these grim figures as an indictment of public policy.

"Government in this area has to be doing what people and families and other organizations can't do on their own," said Bob "Captain Kangaroo" Keeshan, appearing on public television's "MacNeil-Lehrer News Hour" on July 7, 1992. "That's the purpose of government." Keeshan is now a national spokesman for the Coalition for America's Children, comprising more than 170 organizations focusing on children's issues.

"Probably 6 million children go hungry every day," he said. "Probably more than that number are homeless, according to the [CDF] report—they're probably undercounted because we don't find them all in shelters. Many children don't have access to medical care. Poverty is the basic underlying cause of most of these problems, and poverty is really what we have to address. The greatest cure for poverty is jobs and the proper income to strengthen the family."

Yet even the strongest family units have been struggling. We read the news on January 17, 1992: "A congressional study on the incomes of two-parent families confirmed yesterday what most already knew—during the 1980s, they had to run faster just to stay in place." (Washington *Post*)

The study, prepared by the Democratic staff of the Joint Economic Committee, found that two-parent families earned a total of 8 percent more in inflation-adjusted dollars in 1989 than they had in 1979. The rate of growth—less than 1 percent per year—was roughly half what it had been in the 1970s, and one-fifth what it had been in the 1950s. And as small as the growth was, it came from longer hours worked by wives, not from higher wages.

So if you were doing moderately well in the 1980s, you had to work harder and longer just to stay where you were—though at least you weren't going backward. But if you were in the lower reaches of the economic scale, the trend of the last twenty years might have put some of the basic necessities of life tragically beyond your reach.

In our fortunate situation, Joan and I had the means to give Jenny whatever she needed, both materially and emotionally, including the invaluable support of a full-time parent in the home. We did without extras, but far too many American families have had to do without basic needs: without food, shelter, and medical care. How would we feel if it was our child who was going to bed hungry, or who didn't have a decent place to sleep?

The home environment we've been able to give Jenny was once regarded as the norm. For many Americans, it is now beyond their dreams. One of the books in Jenny's library is a story by Dr. Seuss titled *Did I Ever Tell You How Lucky You Are?* It's a serious reminder for all of us, as well as a lifelong lesson for Jenny.

Fathers on Leave

THE "FAMILY LEAVE" CONCEPT may give fathers in the 1990s a real opportunity to be equal parenting partners during their children's early months. Fathers could help ease some of the burdens on working mothers and help answer some of the questions arising from the early use of daycare.

It sounds great, but how many fathers actually would take that chance? From Rochester, New York, came the surprising answer: not many at all.

At its Rochester headquarters, Eastman Kodak has been tracking the number of employees taking advantage of its family leave policy, which grants up to seventeen weeks of unpaid leave for the birth of a child, adoption of a preschool-age child, placement of a preschool-age child in a foster home, or care of a seriously ill family member.

From December 1987 to March 1991, a total of 969 employees took family leave for various lengths of time. Only fifty-four of them were men—just 5.6 percent.

"The participation [by men] is very low," said Kathy Olson, manager of work-life initiatives for Kodak. "But actually, it's higher than a lot of companies that have family leave. In fact, we've gotten a lot of publicity because of it. And *Child* magazine named us one of the thirty best companies for fathers, in large part because of our family leave program."

In assessing the low participation by men, the drop in income with family leave can't be ignored; it is, after all, unpaid leave. Many families would be hard-pressed to do without a paycheck for a month or more. But Olson thought there were other factors involved.

"I think it's still a cultural thing," she said. "The man brings in the money, and he may have a harder time thinking he can be away from his job. I think the guys that take it are seen as real pioneers."

There may not be many men able or willing to do that kind of pioneering, but there also aren't many opportunities. Not many companies embark on "work-life initiatives." According to the

Families and Work Institute in New York, a 1991 survey of Fortune 500 companies showed 28 percent with policies for maternity leave, 22 percent with policies for paternity leave.

If that low figure is surprising, it shouldn't be. The closest the United States has come to a national policy on family leave was the passage of the 1990 Family Leave Act by Congress; that bill, which would have set a standard of twelve weeks of unpaid family leave, was vetoed by President Bush.

Family leave has been gaining momentum at the state level, though. At least twenty-six states, including the District of Columbia, have passed either family-leave laws (twenty states) or maternity-leave laws (six states) in one form or another, and the pace has been accelerating.

The Washington, D.C., Family and Medical Leave Act is regarded as a model for the country: firms with more than fifty employees must grant at least sixteen weeks of unpaid leave during any two-year period for the birth, adoption, or foster-care placement of a child and for serious illness. Job seniority is protected and health insurance must be continued. Language pertaining to sharing a "mutual residence" and a "committed relationship" extends the family leave coverage to gay couples and unmarried heterosexual couples. The law went into effect April 1, 1991; on April 1, 1994, it will apply to companies employing twenty people or more.

Critics of family leave have said that big companies, like Kodak with its 77,000 employees, might well be able to afford family leave, but that the costs are too great for many businesses to bear, especially small businesses.

But a 1991 survey by the Families and Work Institute said that wasn't the case. The institute, a nonprofit research group located in New York, made a three-year study of companies in Minnesota, Wisconsin, Rhode Island, and Oregon, the four states with the longest-standing family-leave laws. The survey, limited to childbirth and adoption-leave cases, showed only 9 percent of the companies had difficulties in complying with their state's leave laws.

The results of the survey (as published in the Los Angeles *Times*) show the effects in three cost categories:

Administrative costs: 6 percent of the companies reported a significant increase; 39 percent reported some increase; 55 percent reported no increase.

Unemployment insurance costs: 2 percent reported a significant increase; 17 percent reported some increase; 81 percent reported no increase.

Health insurance costs: none reported a significant increase; 27 percent reported some increase; 73 percent reported no increase.

There are also plenty of other information sources around the world on how such leave programs might work—especially in Western Europe, where parental and maternity leave have long been in place.

Sweden is always held up as the leading example: each parent can take a leave of a full year, reimbursed at 90 percent of salary. Virtually every other European country has mandated maternity leave: Finland, thirty-five weeks at 100 percent pay; France, eighteen weeks, with sixteen weeks paid at 90 percent; West Germany, at least fourteen weeks at 100 percent; Italy, twenty-two weeks at 60 percent. Both mothers and fathers are eligible for "parental leave" in France (two years with a job guarantee), Germany (eighteen months, minimum pay level with job guarantee) and Italy (six months at 30 percent of wages with job guarantee).

Canada, whose national health-care system has come under close scrutiny in the United States, offers seventeen paid weeks of maternity leave at 60 percent of salary, with an additional twenty-four unpaid weeks for mothers and fathers. Even Japan, so often held up as a model of industrial productivity, has a maternity leave of fourteen paid weeks at 60 percent of salary.

In November 1991, the social ministers of European Community nations agreed on a minimum standard of fourteen weeks' maternity leave at wages at least equal to the sick pay offered in individual countries—far behind Sweden, but a significant benefit to women in countries like Ireland and Portugal, without standard leave policies.

Child care authorities and advocates in the United States have lined up strongly behind the push for a national family leave policy. Harvard University's T. Berry Brazelton thinks the twelve weeks in the 1990 bill that passed Congress should be the minimum.

"There isn't any question in my mind that the first three months have got to be sacred—shorter than that is a sop," said Brazelton (quoted in the Chicago *Sun-Times*). He also favors federally funded daycare and paid family leave.

In the meantime, there are companies like Kodak. Kathy Olson worked with one couple, both Kodak employees, who built up nearly six months of time to be at home with their newborn, by adding maternity leave to alternating months of "his-and-her" family leave followed by "his-and-her" vacation time. And Olson talked with a father who planned to take family leave after the birth of his second child, because he felt he had "missed it all" with his first child, eleven years earlier.

Beyond the shining examples, there is still that disturbingly low proportion of leave-taking fathers. Whether the reason is cultural or economic, we still have a long way to go.

Bags, Bottles, and Books

Bag People On Wheels

ALL BABIES SHOULD BE BORN IN CALIFORNIA. Or all new parents should have the option of spending Year One on the Coast.

To a new parent, housebound in a grim Midwestern winter, the fantasy of California's mellow weather was enticing. With a baby in your arms, your mobility is directly related to the weather. And your sanity is directly related to your mobility.

Imagine tossing away your baby's snowsuit and all the rest of those bulky, hooded-or-hatted wrappings: freedom! Jenny hated being stuffed into those things, no matter how slowly and gently we tried to get them on her. She loved being outdoors, but she hated getting dressed for it, and she let us know how she felt—loud and clear.

Joan and I often were tempted to avoid the hassle of winter dressing for Jenny, but that made us even more housebound. Especially me, with Joan at work much of the day. If the weather turned even a bit mild or sunny, the lure of fresh air was too strong. I'd steel myself to the struggle and dress Jenny. Once we closed the door behind us, the struggle was over. Outdoors, we were reinstated in the world.

But if a winter walk was difficult to stage, a car trip bordered on the impossible. Joan and I divided the preparations. One of us got Jenny ready; the other packed the diaper bag (diaper, diaper covers, changing pad, extra changes of clothes) and the auxiliary bag (toys, amusements, anything else we could think of to toss in at the last minute). If we were escaping for one of our life-saving weekend stays with Joan's mom on the North Side, we also needed our own clothes, toilet kits, books, and any other necessities, though we usually used about half of what we carried.

We would carry the bags, sling them over our shoulders, hang them around our necks. By the time we had the car loaded, we looked like bag people on wheels.

By then, of course, Jenny would be crying. We were invariably late. We had always forgotten something. And secretly, all of us may have been hoping for some last-straw upset so we could cancel the whole trip. But we pushed on, with Joan driving and me in the back seat with Jenny. Joan decided after the first car ride that she got too upset to handle Jenny's road distress, and that became Dad's job for much of the first year.

It was even worse with Jenny's first car seat. A child restraint seat is required by law, and I wouldn't have it any other way. My hair stands on end when I see people driving with a child held in someone's lap—or jumping around without a seat belt on. But Jenny's first car seat drove us all nuts. It was sturdy and well-built. But it was designed for children up to forty pounds, and Jenny weighed just over seven pounds when she was born. We packed her in with blankets, towels, and a head support. We had to dress her, take her out to the car, strap her in the seat, and then strap down the child seat for every trip. Jenny would be screaming, and Joan and I would feel like screaming.

The car seat wasn't just inconvenient: I was sure it was unsafe. For an infant, a car seat is strapped into the rear seat, facing the rear, for maximum safety. But this seat was primarily designed to face forward. When it faced the rear, it simply was not secure: the center of gravity was in the wrong spot, and the seat belt acted as a pivot point, not an anchor. If we had been rear-ended, the child seat could have flipped up and over. It could have bounced Jenny's head into the back of the rear seat, which was not the kind of safety we had in mind.

After two weeks and three car trips, I ripped that seat out of the car, stored it in the garage, and bought another one specifically designed for an infant. Our first seat, I believed, shouldn't be used facing the rear without wedging something underneath to change the angle. Even the manufacturer recognized the flaw; newer models came with a red line added on the side and the statement: "This line must be horizontal (level) when seat is mounted facing rear." I felt vindicated. I wasn't just some crazy, overprotective father.

The new infant seat made car trips simpler, though not necessarily easier. Babies were supposed to love car trips: that's what we were told, but it must only apply to long rides. Toys, music boxes, lullaby tapes, our own talking and singing—nothing worked well in stop-and-go driving. Only a long, continuous ride could get Jenny to settle down and maybe even sleep.

We got a glimpse of paradise during a brief warm spell in March. No winter clothes—and no tears! Just a happy baby looking out the car window, and happy parents singing with relief instead of desperation. And when we walked outside with Jenny, she loved it more than ever. Our world was bigger and happier.

Then the gray cold returned, and we were back to California dreaming. Jenny was born in December; for a long four months, all she knew was winter. Summer could not come quickly enough.

Slow Solutions

WE FOUGHT THE BATTLE OF THE BOTTLE for another month as we dragged through that gray winter. The bottle took a beating, but so did we—all three of us. Under the terms of the peace agreement, the long-term solution was to give breast milk to Jenny in a "sipping cup" with a spout. But even this negotiated settlement did not ease our concerns over Jenny's erratic eating patterns.

Jenny still needed to eat often, sometimes every hour. Her working, nursing mom was often stressed-out by trying to balance Jenny's needs with her own, and trying to pump enough breast milk to meet the minimum daily requirement. Her dad often scrambled to keep her happy, satisfied, or just distracted until Mom got home and nursing time could resume.

Some babies may adapt happily to a feeding schedule: not Jenny. For most of her first five-and-a-half months, she fed as if she were in a constant growth spurt, with some justification. She weighed seven pounds, one ounce and was twenty inches long at birth; at twenty-four weeks, she weighed fourteen pounds and was more than twenty-six inches long. She essentially doubled her weight and increased her length by one-third. In her fifth month, she gained nineteen ounces. She practically grew before our eyes.

It was all done on breast milk, with one short diversion.

During a warm spell in April, when Jenny was four months old, we were concerned about maintaining her fluid levels. She was still ambivalent toward breast milk in a cup, so we were advised to try diluted apple juice.

Jenny liked it, but she had a funny reaction. She would be satisfied for a few minutes, then begin crying as if the apple juice actually made her hungrier. Here's why: apple juice is a simple carbohydrate, almost entirely fructose, and it is immediately turned into sugar in the body. Jenny's blood sugar level would soar, then plummet because of her body's increased insulin production. This is the same effect produced by a candy bar. We stopped the apple juice immediately. But we still had to get her to take enough milk to meet her needs.

We couldn't forget our own needs. Without a dependable alternate feeding method, Joan and I could not break away for dinner or a movie. We couldn't even count on eating a normal dinner at home, or having time to talk. Joan could not go to work without fearing that Jenny would be hungry.

The most common solution is to switch to formula. We never seriously considered it.

"From everything I've read and learned," Joan said, "breastfeeding is the best for Jenny. It's best for her nutrition, for developing her digestive system, for developing her immunities, for preventing food allergies. I never realized how much of a commitment this would be. But I want what's best for her. I'll breastfeed her no matter how difficult it is."

Our one mistake might have been waiting until Jenny was eleven weeks old to introduce the bottle. She was enraged by the bottle and the nipple. Then again, knowing the strength of Jenny's will, she might have fought off this poor substitute for Joan no matter when we introduced it. And I was not willing to let her get screamingly hungry enough to take the bottle out of desperation—another tactic that was suggested to us.

At sixteen weeks, I tried the cup. Jenny was not happy, but neither did she try to knock the cup out of sight, as she had with the bottle. She would take some milk, but her conscious swallowing skill was still relatively undeveloped. More milk poured back out of her mouth than stayed in it.

Now I'll take credit for a good idea. I looked for a cup with one hole in the spout instead of three or four, thinking it might be less confusing for her if less milk came pouring out. I also wanted the cup to have two handles, so she could hold onto it.

I found precisely that cup, and Jenny adapted right away. She took the handles and tried to put the spout to her mouth. Sometimes she hit herself in the nose or the eye, or poured milk in her ear. But within three or four weeks, she was practically feeding herself from the cup, with a little guidance from me.

Even with the cup, she seldom went more than two hours without eating. She was still a "grazer." And when Joan was available, Jenny seldom went longer than an hour between feedings.

Solid food (rice cereal) was scheduled to be the next step, but we wanted to hold off until Jenny was six months old. We wanted to be sure her digestive system was mature enough to handle the more complex food, to lessen the chances of stomach problems and food allergies.

We were determined to stick by our beliefs in what was best for Jenny. We told ourselves that life really would become easier, if we were just patient until we got to that next stage. But time could be a slow solution.

Reading With Jenny

THERE ARE MANY BOOKS I remember more clearly than *War Paint*, but none I remember more fondly.

War Paint, the story of a Native American boy and his beloved pony, was my favorite book long before I could read. It was a tall book with a yellow cover, and on its thick pages were large line drawings of the boy, his people, and the horse, War Paint. My mom read the story to me at bedtime as I followed those wonderful drawings. I remember little about the story itself, but the memory of that early reading experience is indelible.

War Paint, that treasured book that has long been lost in time, opened the door to reading and learning for me. Without it, my life might not have been the same. There might not have been any of my long afternoon walks to the library, returning with an armload of books while mentally scheduling a way to read them all in the next two weeks before they were due. I might never have met Sherlock Holmes or Horatio Hornblower; never have discovered Thomas Wolfe or Ernest Hemingway; never have enjoyed Red Smith or Rex Stout; never have appreciated Raymond Chandler or Robertson Davies. Without *War Paint*, I might have missed so much.

Maybe that's why I began reading to Jenny so early, hoping to help her open that door to a life of books.

It was probably silly to try reading some of Anne Tyler's *Dinner at the Homesick Restaurant* to Jenny when she was a week old. She wasn't much interested, and we didn't get past the first page. What can I say? I had run out of things to do and the paperback was handy.

Joan, who loves books as much as I do, made Jenny's first real reading connection. She was sitting with Jenny in her rocking chair a few weeks later when she decided to read Maurice Sendak's *Where the Wild Things Are*. Jenny was intrigued by the colorfully drawn wild things, and followed along as Joan turned the pages. Jenny also liked Margaret Wise Brown's classic *Good Night,*

Moon. She might not stay tuned in for the entire story, but she would usually be interested for at least a little while.

Then, on a Saturday morning when Jenny was ten weeks old, Joan decided to try a favorite of her own: one of A. A. Milne's little volumes of children's poems, *Now We Are Six*. Joan began to read "King Hilary and the Beggarman," and Jenny's face was alight. She smiled with her eyes as well as her mouth, and burbled back at the rhymes, the rhythms, and the repetitions. And Jenny loved to look at the woodcut drawings, eagerly shifting her focus as the pages were turned.

We were delighted: We had a daughter who liked books! We could read with Jenny!

Our one overriding hope for Jenny always has been that she would love to read. I was glad for any source of information that offered encouragement, such as a psychological study showing that children of readers tended to become readers themselves (even among twins separated at an early age). On Jenny's first Christmas, my gift to her was a book.

From her earliest days, we were eager for any hint that Jenny liked stories or books. When I walked around the house with Jenny on my shoulder, she always seemed interested in the bookcases. It was a nice little fantasy that she already loved books. More likely, she was drawn by the repeated strong parallel lines, the range of colors, and the strong contrasts provided by the print of the titles. Yet I remember watching her at sixteen weeks as she scanned the bookcases in my office, taking them all into her gaze, almost as if browsing in her own library.

We pictured Jenny absorbed in the wonders of reading, on special days like the ones Joan knew as a little girl. Joan would receive books as Christmas presents and then lie on the rug in front of the fire, entranced with her own world of words for the rest of the day. Sometimes I imagined Jenny lying warm near our own fireplace, a book propped in front of her, her chin resting in her hands, off on her own journey.

We've read to Jenny virtually every day of her life, often sharing story after story, sometimes reading the same story two or three times in a row. I hope that encouraging her never leads to pushing her. We are not trying to create a "super-achiever" with a reading score off the chart before she starts school. We simply hope Jenny can share the joy we have found in reading. Our books are like our truest friends, and some of our earliest friends remain our best friends. The "My Book House" books that taught Joan to read are still with her. The set is in our special bookcase, along with my treasured Hornblower saga. And with them, waiting, is Jenny's first Christmas book, with a message from Dad on the first page.

I hope some book will reach Jenny the way *War Paint* reached me. A world of books is waiting for her.

A Mother's Day
(Written for Mother's Day, 1990)

AFTER A DAY OF DEALING WITH BANK BALANCES, marketing strategy, and personnel management for her company, Joan came home and began inspecting the refrigerator.

"There's something about being a mother," she said, "that makes me think about a healthy dinner at the end of the day. I know I have to eat well so Jenny will eat well."

Joan isn't simply a working mother. She is a working, nursing mother. Jenny depends on her for nourishment as well as nurturing. That means Jenny is seldom far from Joan for any length of time, and she is never out of Joan's thoughts from the moment she wakes until she falls asleep.

No day is exactly like another day, but a mother's day goes something like this when she's nursing and working:

Jenny usually awakens at around 7:00 A.M., though sometimes as early at 5:45. Whatever the time, Joan is awake moments earlier, waiting. When Jenny has finished stretching and smiling her "Good mornings" to us, Joan begins nursing her for her "first breakfast." She reads to Jenny, then showers quickly, dresses quickly, and breakfasts quickly. Everything done for yourself is done quickly when you have a baby. Joan nurses Jenny again, then she's off to work, hoping Jenny isn't still hungry.

"It's real hard to be away from her when I think she might be hungry," Joan says. "And it's a combination of a lot of reactions—physical, emotional, and hormonal. It's a very strong feeling."

Joan always manages at least one checkup call in the morning. Jenny never would accept a bottle of breast milk, and wouldn't take breast milk from a cup with any dependability. So Joan comes home from her nearby office for lunch each day—her own lunch, and Jenny's lunch. And usually, Jenny's second lunch. Then it's back to work for the afternoon, repeating the checkups by phone.

After work, Joan and Jenny have a big reunion, overflowing with smiles, hugs, and kisses. Joan wants to make sure Jenny can make up for the lost time, the missed closeness, of the work day. The evenings can be as tiring as the days, but the simplest of shared times can bring the greatest rewards, whether taking a bath together before bedtime, or just taking a walk to the park to see the springtime blossoms.

"One day I was showing Jenny all the beautiful flowers," Joan said. "We were standing under a great flowering tree, in a canopy of blossoms and fragrance. I was babbling to her about all the beauty around us, and she became so involved. She was gleeful. I experienced such joy, sharing all the beauty with this little person I love so much."

As much as we learn about her, Jenny offers us a constant opportunity to learn about ourselves. We thought we had so many answers, after waiting until our forties to become parents. Far from it.

"I had reached the point where I felt I had conquered so many things about my life," Joan said. "I could manage things so well, so smoothly. I felt so much more whole as a person. I felt that I could be a good mother. The decision to have a child was such a conscious one, not like it would have been when I was in my twenties and having a child was simply what you did.

"But having a child now has been like going back to square one. I've found out how much I don't know. I have so much more to learn about myself. There are so many more vulnerabilities. So many memories come back from my own childhood, both happy and sad."

There is also that matter of successfully managing a life and having it go smoothly. A baby is always inviting you to change your plans.

"By the end of the week, I feel completely exhausted," Joan said. "But even the chaos really has a positive quality. I would never have had the chance to become the person I feel I could become, without this wonderful little child that I'm so closely bonded to. Having your own child to love is a privilege. That's exactly the way I feel. It is such a privilege."

Becoming a mother, and receiving her own mother's guidance, also deepened Joan's feelings of privilege about being a daughter.

"I couldn't love my mom any more than I do," she said. "But I have a new respect for her. She's really my heroine. She raised seven children with such love and care. She's still there for all of us, with love, with wisdom, as a friend and as a mother."

Jenny may already sense that she is as fortunate as Joan. She's going to have her own heroine for a mom.

Early Steps, Early Messages

Jenny didn't believe in learning to crawl before she learned to walk. Crawling was too slow for her. She wanted to walk, and the sooner the better. We never expected it so early, but her first attempt came when she was eighteen weeks old. Joan was playing with her, doing "baby situps": holding her hands and helping her pull herself up into a sitting position. Jenny couldn't sit up on her own, but she loved being upright. I tried it later, on the rug, and Jenny didn't want to stop at sitting. She stiffened her legs, kept pulling until she was standing, and tried to walk up my lap.

On a Saturday morning a week later, we were doing more situps on the rug. Jenny kept pulling herself up until she was standing. She put out her left foot, then followed with her right. Suddenly, if unsteadily, she was walking. She took ten steps while I held her up by her hands, and she didn't want to quit. Her legs were wobbly, but not her spirit.

Joan and I were as thrilled as we were surprised, but we didn't want to push Jenny into something she wasn't ready to do. How would we know how much to encourage her?

Jenny soon gave us the answer. Lying on her back, she began reaching out with both arms, grasping for our hands. She couldn't have said "Pull me up!" more clearly.

So Jenny began spending a lot of time on her feet, astonishing us with the sight of our little girl standing up and enjoying her new view of her world. Her walking tired us out more than it tired her. I actually got rug burn on my knees. What she lacked in strength and coordination, she made up for with her determination and spirit. After every attempt, we gave her enthusiastic applause. We called it Jenny's "standing ovation."

She loved the clapping. She replied with a smile, sometimes with a laugh. It had to be gratifying to her, and not just because she suddenly could put one foot in front of the other.

Of course, she was not yet ready to walk; many children take these early, tentative steps when walking is still months away.

What was going on with her feet was less important than what was going on with her mind.

Consider all the thinking Jenny had to put into this achievement. After more than four months of lying around and being carried, she decided she wanted to move in a different way. She set her goals: she wanted to stand up and move. She had to understand the concept of putting one foot in front of the other. She had to understand the concept of moving through space. She had to have a sense of her own body, and a sense of her own identity, separate from all the things around her.

She still had another problem to solve: how to deal with her complete dependence on us, how to get us to help her achieve her goal of movement. Her solution: reaching up to us, and getting us to reach down to her and pull her up. She collated her experiences of being held by us, and of touching and grasping the things around her—including us. And she communicated with us.

As much as that message meant to us, imagine what it meant to Jenny. For more than four months, all the lifetime she knew, her basic means of communication was crying. That was how she let us know about her needs, and we weren't always able to understand those needs.

But now she had communicated her wants to us—and wants are a step up in complexity from needs, such as hunger. She had communicated, we had understood, and we had responded immediately in the way she wanted us to respond. In a basic way, she had interacted with us on our own level.

Reaching up was not her first communication of that kind. At around sixteen weeks, as I carried her around the house, Jenny began telling me when she wanted to stop and look at something. "Ah," she said, very specifically. "Ah. Ah." The first time, she wanted to examine a ceramic figure atop a low bookcase. The next time, it was a colorful piece of Joan's pottery. She smiled when I brought her closer for a better look, her eyes locked on her target.

And she communicated in yet another way: with her laughter. She showed that she understood humor, from a funny face or a funny noise; she clearly understood fun, from being hoisted above our heads, or kicking her feet in the bath, or being assaulted with kisses. Her laughter was charming and infectious, and I hope it will always serve to balance her seriousness of purpose. Jenny was not simply a baby any longer. She was becoming a child, a little person developing a full and complex personality.

Each day was a new discovery for our determined but fun-loving little girl, who wanted to walk before she could crawl. We may have seen the beginning of her pattern for life. I just hope we can keep up with her.

Those Baby Books

HERE ARE TWO PRACTICAL TIPS FROM DR. SPOCK: slip clothing over the back of a baby's head, not the top; and take your watch off before giving a baby a bath.

Thank you, Dr. Spock. That will be all.

That's the key to using those big, encyclopedic baby books: knowing when to put them down. Baby books can be an invaluable resource, especially for medical information and particularly if new parents are isolated from the support of family and friends. Baby books can also threaten your sanity.

The bookshelves are full of them, especially the "Big Three" of Penelope Leach, T. Berry Brazelton, and the venerable Benjamin Spock. The baby manuals give you guidelines on mental and physical development, clothing, feeding, sleeping, learning, and disciplining. What they lack are guidelines on using their guidelines, so I have come up with five rules of thumb for dealing with baby experts and their books:

1. Nobody is really sure what goes on inside a baby for those chaotic first three months of life, and babies can't read what the experts say is going on.

2. That expert on babies never met your baby. You are the expert on your baby. The "average baby" featured in most manuals is probably a robot.

3. Few experts show much understanding of what goes on inside a parent, especially a first-time parent desperate for reassurance. You can feel like a freak when you're in a panic and the book has no section dealing with panic—or even hinting that panic is a possibility.

4. Be willing, at any time, to pitch a baby manual against the wall or out the window. The confusion and fatigue that go with real-life baby care can have little resemblance to the detached and orderly instructions between those glossy covers.

5. Try to envision the expert as a baby who soiled his diapers, didn't follow the rules, and had his parents absolutely frazzled. It will help your perspective.

I remember flinging Leach's *Your Baby and Child* across the room when I came across a pie chart showing how easy it was to "merge" feedings and establish a convenient schedule. Jenny wanted to nurse virtually every waking hour most of her first three months. Joan was exhausted, but continued nursing according to Jenny's needs.

Ours wasn't the only clash with an expert, or the most infuriating. Close friends of ours trashed Spock after reading that they should let their distraught child lie in proximity to her own vomit, and not clean it up until after she went to sleep (Section 348 of *Baby and Child Care*—including the revised 1985 edition). Did it ever occur to Spock that, if a child is vomiting at bedtime, it might be wise for the parents to step back and reconsider their whole approach? Did it ever occur to him that there might be some other way to do this without inciting a nightly crisis? If you're sticking with Spock on this issue, you could be pretty stuck.

But the huge popularity of baby-care books points to a crying need for information. Why? Because the old-time extended family has gone the way of black-and-white television.

Babies no longer have grandparents, aunts and uncles around all the time to pick them up, play with them, and give tired parents a break. Parents seldom have Mom living within shouting distance, or a sister with her own children living a few blocks away—or even in the same town. Some of the best sources on well-baby care can be a living reference book in the person of a loving grandparent, or a sympathetic ear and a helpful hand from a sister who just went through something similar with her own child. Now the family is smaller, and usually extended only by distance. Whoever invented the nuclear family wasn't motivated by child care.

So we go buy the books, for guidance from the basic (folding a diaper) to the ambitious (producing a genius child). Even *Esquire* magazine ran a spread in November 1989, on "How to Raise a Perfect Kid," among its Porsche and BMW ads.

What do we want from baby books? More than just information. We want confirmation of our own feelings on child care. We want to hear someone who sounds like us. If we want things neat and orderly, we probably won't buy the work of an expert who counsels constant attention and constant contact. If we want our child in-arms, we won't stand for "shut the door and let the baby cry it out alone."

Then there are the special cases. Joan and I latched onto Dr. William Sears' *The Fussy Baby* when Jenny seemed overwhelmed by distress and cried constantly. None of the other manuals we read dealt with such a high-need baby. Sears advised holding and comforting Jenny as much as possible, which we already were doing; and trying to anticipate her needs, by heightening our own sense of involvement. We may have listened closely because Sears' approach seemed an extension of our own. Yet we found that even Sears had his limitations, and we had to seek some of our own solutions to the difficulties posed by the circumstance of a highly sensitive baby with a working, nursing mother.

A baby book can truly be a lifeline if we are isolated from support and medical advice. Everyone needs help. But we still have to live our own questions, and discover our own answers. Ultimately, we write our own book, for our own baby.

The 1992 Sears Catalogue for Children and Families

IF YOU WANT TO TALK TO DR. WILLIAM SEARS, you have to get used to the sound of children in the background.

"I'm holding our three-month-old right now," said Sears, speaking by telephone from his home near San Clemente, California.

Sears and his wife, Martha, have eight children. Lauren, the youngest, who was nestling in Sears' arms, was adopted as a newborn.

"Whenever Martha sees something about overpopulation," Sears said, "she just says: 'The world needs my kids.'"

Sears also believes many kids need more from their world. When he wrote *The Fussy Baby*, he left little doubt about his advocacy of a prolonged nurturing relationship between a baby and its parents. But he said *The Baby Book*, his soon-to-be-completed sixteenth volume on child care, would make an even stronger case.

"It is not a wimpy book," he said.

Central to Sears' thinking are his doubts about the system of child care that seems, without any sort of plan, to be emerging in America. He is firmly on the side of Penelope Leach, who believes that the best place for infants during their critical first year is in the home, with a parent or another consistent primary caregiver, where infants can be the focus of attention. Leach believes in the social benefits of group activities such as daycare, but also believes they are most valuable when they are introduced at a somewhat later stage of development.

"I give Penelope Leach credit for having the courage to say what's true," said Sears, "regardless of whether it's politically correct or not . . . Penelope Leach and others are saying, 'Let's take a look at this, and let's quit fooling ourselves.'"

Sears' major concern is the outlook on life that may be instilled when a child doesn't receive enough one-on-one attention in the crucial early months, an outlook that may leave a child short on understanding the nature of caring. He believes the early use of daycare has become accepted as the norm without a clear enough picture of its long-range consequences.

"Psychologists say that studies show kids are OK in day care. But if you look carefully, what they're studying is strictly performance—not attitudes, not what I call 'sensitivity.' If a child is used to being nurtured, to being held, to being cared about—that forms a life-long attitude. I'm afraid we're creating a generation of insensitive kids."

Sears views economics as the crux of the question. He points to the crunch caused by the decline in family income in the last two decades, and the necessity for both parents to hold jobs—if a family is lucky enough to include both parents. "We need the easing of financial pressures on families. Maybe we're more aware of it in California, but it's almost necessary to have two incomes."

Sears is impatient with what he calls "pro-family rhetoric." He'd like to see a closer connection made between rhetoric and policy.

"In our current system everybody wins except the babies. Somebody in high places, or some advocacy group, has to get going and say, 'Hey, our current system isn't working.' The government has got to realize the importance of keeping families together during the child's first year."

Sears also would like to see a sort of "cultural fix" in our attitude toward early child care. "I think the main thing is that mothers are not fully convinced of their importance to a baby. Nor are fathers. Take an issue like breastfeeding—I think many mothers don't breastfeed their babies because they're just not convinced of the importance of doing it. But that's going to change."

Sears has seen one important change through his work as a pediatrician. He acknowledges that fathers have become more involved in raising their children.

"I think they are, if for no other reason than out of necessity. As more and more mothers work outside the home, fathers are being brought into the home. It's the only good effect I've seen of mothers leaving their babies. If mothers have to share in the income, then fathers have to share in child care.

"But I've also seen it in what I call the 'second-time around dad.'

It's his second marriage, her first. He's going to do it right this time. He doesn't have to climb the corporate ladder. He missed [the involvement] in his first time around, and he's not going to miss it on the second time around."

Yet Sears is also aware that fathers remain an underutilized resource in child care. He understands there are probably financial reasons underlying the apparently poor response of fathers in a large company offering paternity leave, like Kodak.

"It could just be a question of economics, where they can't afford to be without any income . . . but I don't think the father is convinced of the importance to the development of the baby and to himself. If he was truly convinced of the importance, he would probably take the time. As we see in economics, if one is fully convinced of the importance to do something, one will find a way to do it."

Sears would like more fathers to be convinced of the importance, and more mothers, too. He'd like our society to get more accustomed to the sound of children in the background.

"If we have created a system where we can't afford to care for our children," says Dr. William Sears, "our future is in jeopardy."

A Father's Job

A Father's Job
(Written for Father's Day, 1990)

JOAN'S DOCTOR was good at giving a needle.

"How does it feel to be a mom?" she asked on one of our visits—but she wasn't asking Joan.

She was asking me, and I felt just a little bit stung. But I forced a smile, hiked my voice up a couple of octaves, and said, "Oh, it's simply wonderful!"

At one time, I would have gotten angrily defensive over that kind of teasing. But after six months as an at-home father, I had gained a perspective that allowed me to view with amusement the condescending remarks of people who failed to understand and appreciate what I was doing.

Or maybe, at this point, I was just too tired to argue.

Being home with Jenny every day was the hardest job I've ever had. There were no breaks, but the physical pace of keeping up with an alert, exuberant and nonstop child wasn't even the hardest half of the work. The mental demands were exhausting. I could never stop thinking. Each minute might require a new decision or a new judgment.

I could not coast through a bad day on automatic pilot, not when it might take all my skills of observation to decode Jenny's needs. I could not slide by with a half-effort, just watching the clock until I hopped on the train to head home at the end of the day. I was always home, and the work day had no end, not even when Joan came home from her job. Because Jenny still had a long way to go before sleep.

Don't ever tell me someone is "just" a mom. But that same kind of judgment was often made of me. Caring for a child didn't seem to be enough for someone to do. I was often asked, either directly or by implication: "What else do you do? Is that it?" Yes, it was sometimes hard to explain, even to myself, how keeping up with a such a small child could fill such a long day. On a good day, I took a shower and got the laundry done. On a great day, I took a shower, got the laundry done, and found ten peaceful minutes in the bathroom with the book I'd been trying to read one page at a time for the last month.

And I am a *man*: being home with a child was such a curious thing for a man to do. How could it possibly be enough of a challenge for a man? That judgment often seemed to hang just behind the smile when someone decided to give me a job title: "housedaddy," "full-time babysitter," and, of course, "Mr. Mom."

None of those titles sounded very complimentary, and being called "Mr. Mom" really used to aggravate me. But I decided that, in our society, a film can legitimize an idea: "Hey, I saw a guy like you in the movies!" So if a movie made it easier for someone to digest the idea of a man caring for a child, why argue? Besides, Michael Keaton went from playing "Mr. Mom" to "Batman." Who knows what the future might hold?

I hope the future will hold a different value judgment of child care. The job pays nothing, and that creates a lot of confusion. When we say "value," we usually mean "money." If a job doesn't pay any money, how can it have any value? If a man—and especially a man—isn't making money, what is the value of his effort?

I fell into that trap myself. I didn't decide to stay home with Jenny as a crusade for men's liberation. I wasn't trying to change the world. I wanted what was best for her, but I thought caring for a child would simply add a few interruptions to a day's work.

Instead, it became the entire day's work. When other jobs were not completed, or not even begun, I got frustrated and felt as if I wasn't accomplishing anything important. After all, staying home meant I wasn't making nearly the money I had once made.

That was the confusion between money and value, between pay and reward.

I had to ask myself: how many dollars equaled one of Jenny's smiles? How many paychecks equaled her laughter, or her squeals of delight when I hoisted her over my head? Where could Joan and I buy the satisfaction of knowing that Jenny was in her own home each day, with one of her parents there to care for her? When I asked myself those questions, I knew where the greatest value was for Jenny and for us.

So I decided you could call me whatever you wanted. I was trying to call myself a good father. I know I'm a lucky one.

TV Dads Weren't All Tube Boobs

WE'VE KNOWN FOR MORE THAN FORTY YEARS that a man could take care of children.

Television taught us.

Go back to 1952, the days of big, heavy TV sets with the little black-and-white screens, when investment executive Vern Albright (Charles Farrell) would laugh with resignation and pronounce: "Well, that's my little Margie!"

It wasn't the first time a widower assumed the sole responsibility of bringing up his child, but "My Little Margie" was the first example in TV history. And in his own way, Vern Albright was ahead of his time.

When twenty-one-year-old Margie (Gale Storm) wanted to discuss something serious, she'd glance over her shoulder and tell Vern: "I'm sure glad Dad isn't around."

Vern would make the switch, and Vern-as-mom always listened differently to Margie. Instead of saying "Margie, stop this nonsense," he was calmer, more sympathetic, more understanding, more willing to see a question through Margie's eyes. Maybe Vern had to play "mom" to show his nurturing side, but he did have a nurturing side to show. He was a surprisingly complete parent for his time.

Starting with Vern Albright, "solo dads" were regular primetime entries in the 1950s and 1960s: "Bachelor Father," "Family Affair," "Bonanza," "My Three Sons," "The Andy Griffith Show."

But it wasn't until 1969 that a show reprised the idea of a father who carefully and regularly listened to his child.

Magazine publisher Tom Corbett (a pre-Hulk Bill Bixby) was the widowed father of seven-year-old Eddie in "The Courtship of Eddie's Father." In an epilogue to each episode, Eddie talked about some part of his growing understanding of the world. Tom listened, and you knew he was savoring every word.

"Eddie's Father" was special, focusing more on the relationship between father and child than virtually any other TV "solo dad" show (and more than the 1963 movie with Glenn Ford and Ronnie Howard). Bill Bixby's Tom Corbett might well have been the TV prototype of the sensitive, nurturing father now held up as a model in the 1990s. But even he fit the mold of a solo dad in an accidental situation.

Most of the TV dads were widowers—Vern Albright, Tom Corbett, Andy Taylor of "The Andy Griffith Show," three-time widower Ben Cartwright (Lorne Greene) of "Bonanza," and Steve Douglas (Fred MacMurray) of "My Three Sons."

Other dads had families that were "inherited:" Hollywood lawyer Bentley Gregg (John Forsythe) became a "Bachelor Father" after his thirteen-year-old niece, Kelly, was orphaned by a car crash; consulting engineer Bill Davis (Brian Keith) inherited three children (including six-year-old twins) to begin his "Family Affair."

Only one solo dad made a conscious choice, and that was in 1955 on "Fury." Jim Newton (Peter Graves), who was single, adopted a troubled boy named Joey (Bobby Diamond) and brought him to the Broken Wheel Ranch. To teach Joey about responsibility, Jim presented him with a black stallion named Fury.

For a fairly minor show, "Fury" also was a pioneer in another area: housework. Pete (William Fawcett), who spent equal time in apronstrings and on horseback, may have been the prototype of the crotchety male housekeeper trying to keep order.

Other TV dads had housekeepers of a different kind. Bentley Gregg had a "houseboy" named Peter (Sammee Tong). Bill Davis had Giles French (Sebastian Cabot), an English "gentleman's gentleman." Andy Taylor had both Aunt Bea and the entire town of Mayberry helping him and Opie. Even Tom Corbett had the amusing and tender Mrs. Livingston (Myoshi Umeki) to keep his household running.

The ornery male housekeeper reached a pinnacle in "My Three Sons," with Steve Douglas' father-in-law, Bub O'Casey (William Frawley), and later, Bub's brother, Uncle Charley O'Casey (William Demarest) taking on the apron and vacuum. But the endurance record (fourteen years, 1959–73) belonged to Hop Sing (Victor Sen Young) who rode herd on the Cartwrights indoors. Hop Sing would have made an ideal "wife": he coped with all that dust and dirt, always had meals on the table and clean clothes on the Cartwright boys, and apparently had no life of his own. However, Hop Sing had to be ecstatic that he wasn't a woman, given Ben's marital history.

No TV dad coped with housework on a regular basis until Tony Micelli (Tony Danza) actually worked as a housekeeper on "Who's The Boss?" (1984). What's more, he was employed by two women—another breakthrough. Tony was a widower bringing up his daughter, Samantha; he was also a former professional ballplayer, a step toward a more macho identity for the solo dad. Following up was TV sportscaster Danny Tanner (Bob Saget), who ran a "Full House" of three men and three children starting in 1987.

With TV dads leading the way in our consciousness—and with economic upheavals banging home some harsh truths—we were well prepared for Michael Keaton taking over the house and kids in the movie *Mr. Mom*, even if it was only temporarily, while he was unemployed and wife Teri Garr was flashing through an ad agency like a comet.

And it wasn't so outrageous for T.S. Garp to stay home and write while taking care of his children. In fact, it was engaging enough to help turn John Irving's *The World According to Garp* into a best-seller and a successful movie starring Robin Williams.

The solo dad formula also worked when it was multiplied in *Three Men and a Baby*—the outlandish situation of men caring for an abandoned infant, with their pratfalls, their growth into real "parents," their coming to terms with the baby's mother (and, in *Three Men and a Little Lady*, the tortuous process of getting the baby's mother married to soft-hearted hunk Tom Selleck).

We saw how much was at stake for a father and child in the aftermath of a divorce in the landmark movie *Kramer vs. Kramer*, with Dustin Hoffman gaining custody of his son and reconstructing—if not reinventing—their lives and their relationship. Five Academy Awards for 1979 (including Best Picture and Best Actor for Hoffman) offered powerful testimony in support of a nurturing father.

By now, we've also been treated to an array of real-life personalities who have suddenly discovered, in their middle age, that they are mesmerized by fathering: legendary bachelor Warren Beatty, Jack Nicholson, Richard Pryor, Robin Williams, even that immortal playboy Hugh Hefner.

The evolution of the solo dad in TV and film has had the effect of taking what was once a curiosity and bringing it into the accepted range of normality. It has taken the idea of a man caring for a child and evolved it from a comic premise (where we are laughing at the dad) into a humorous one (where we are laughing with the dad). The solo dad has been brought into the fold of society; he is in our consciousness, identified with the reality we know best—the reality of the screen, big or little.

So today if a man is caring for a child, he may be greeted with a laugh and called "Mr. Mom." If he is regarded with humor, at least he is no longer a target for ridicule.

Thanks to TV.

Cosby and the Captain

As A KID, I thought Captain Kangaroo was dumb. As an adult, I thought Bill Cosby was cool.

But I began second-guessing myself after reading their books on parenting: Cosby's *Fatherhood*, first published in 1986, and Bob "Captain Kangaroo" Keeshan's *Growing Up Happy*, issued in September 1989.

Cosby became America's most visible and probably most influential father (and one of its wealthiest), thanks to the popularity of "The Cosby Show." But while his TV kids were presented as real, complex people, his own kids are comic targets in his book.

In real life, Cosby surely loves his five children. But does he like them? That's the surprising question I kept asking myself. Maybe I was disappointed in Cosby's description of the birth of his first child, when he says he told his wife: "Darling, I love you very much. You just had a lizard."

On TV, Cosby sometimes got his comeuppance. In the book, he is infallible, and his kids are idiots: "We have always been against calling the children idiots," he writes. "This philosophy has been basic for my wife and me. And we proudly lived by it until the children came along."

Peel back the surface, and no doubt there's a full layer of emotion. It's based in male-bonding style, honed in the locker room, with a message that may be saying: "If I didn't care about you, would I spend so much time dumping on you and making fun of you?" But how would you like your father to tell several million readers you were an idiot?

Maybe it worked for Cosby. But he never seemed to use his remarkable creativity in trying to understand his own kids. And did he enjoy doing anything with them? His recurrent theme is looking forward to the day when all his kids have moved out, and dreading the possibility any of them might move back in.

If *Fatherhood* sounded like standup comedy, that's essentially what it was. *The New York Times Book Review* described writer Ralph Schoenstein putting the book together from tapes and notes of conversations with Cosby; much of the material originated in Cosby's comedy routines.

It may not be enough to redeem the book, but Cosby does offer some practical advice. There are no absolute rules when it comes to raising children, he said: "You just need a lot of love and luck—and, of course, courage because you'll be spending many years in fear of your kids." Both parents must be consistent with their decisions, he says, especially in imposing discipline. And: "No matter how he talks, a father cannot sound hip to his children."

Captain Kangaroo didn't sound hip to me when I first visited his TV Treasure House nearly thirty-five years ago. Why would he want to do things like cuddle a dumb, ugly rabbit? If I wanted rabbits, Bugs Bunny's wisecracking style was a lot closer to my experience on the New York City streets. Yet the gentle Keeshan had been a city kid himself.

Now I felt I missed something by not watching the Captain more often. I hoped he'd be around long enough for Jenny to share his warmth and decency. And his humor.

Keeshan's stories are invariably funnier than Cosby's. With all the confusion children experience and create, they are easy comic targets. But Keeshan laughs with them, not at them, as in a story about his neighbor's children. When they came home from preschool, their mom told them their dog, Patty, was hit by a car and killed. The children, unmoved, went out to play but later became upset when they called for Patty and the dog didn't answer. Mom repeated the news about Patty. "Oh," they wailed through tears. "We thought you said 'Daddy.'"

Hardship may have been a source of Keeshan's understanding nature. He was fired as Clarabell the Clown on the "Howdy Doody" show in 1953, when he and his wife were expecting their second child. Keeshan resorted to rounding up empty soda bottles for the two-cent deposit on each, "and some weeks that meant being able to pay for groceries."

Sure, the Captain can be exasperating when he sends up a platitude without an example to back it up. But he holds a clear and compelling viewpoint throughout: "Many a parent-child struggle results from the parent's inability to see the situation from the child's perspective. It is necessary to step outside yourself, to put yourself in the small shoes of the child and EMPATHIZE." Maybe sounding hip isn't so important.

Fatherhood may give parents a laugh at night when the kids finally are asleep after a tough day. But *Growing Up Happy* will keep you in touch with treating and respecting your child as a little person. Cosby won't be doing any babysitting for us, but the Captain can visit Jenny any time.

The Second Shift

How many fathers are actually at home with their kids?

Chris Stafford guesses there are about a million, but he isn't sure. He knows that he's one of them, but tracking down others is haphazard.

Stafford left a job and a career to be an at-home father while his wife returned to work. But there is also an "at-home" attitude among some fathers who don't give up their jobs. They do more than give "quality time" to their children; after their jobs, they also work a second shift in child care. That makes them different.

In *The Second Shift: Working Parents and the Revolution at Home* (Viking Penguin, 1989), Arlie Hochschild and Anne Machung found that working women were seriously disappointed, if not angered and disillusioned, by the low level of support they received from their husbands in household and child-care responsibilities. The women said that after they worked a full day at their jobs, they also worked a "second shift" at home in caring for their young children. A study by Hochschild (a sociologist at the University of California-Berkeley) showed that only 20 percent of the husbands matched their wives' efforts on this second shift.

But not Jim Kelley and Joe Novotny, who are veterans of the second shift. With Chris Stafford, they furnish the true stories of three men and their babies.

Daddy, the Publisher

Chris Stafford has been an at-home father for eleven years. But at forty-two, with both children in school, he has decided it's time to go back to work.

"Now I'm facing an issue that women have been facing for years," he said, "giving a prospective employer a resume that says you took ten years off from work to raise your children."

Chris' wife, Barbara, is a regional manager for an insurance company. Chris wasn't completely out of touch with the job market while being home in New Brighton, Minnesota, with Meghan, now eleven, and Ryan, seven. From April 1991 to January 1992, he published a newsletter called *Full-Time Dads*.

"We had about 400 subscribers nationwide, from very, very different backgrounds," he said, "They ranged from attorneys to a garbage truck driver who had been disabled on the job.

"We published every other month, and I sent out five issues. I lost a lot of money on it. I was always certain it would be a real tough 'go.' When I started out, I set a dollar figure and said that was the limit of what I could lose. As soon as I reached that figure, I had to stop.

"But I know a couple of the major publishers started magazines for fathers and they only lasted one issue. I did five issues. At least I'll always have the satisfaction of knowing I outlasted some of the big guys."

His biggest problem with the newsletter was numbers: there didn't seem to be any way to find numbers on fathers who were at home and caring for their children, or who had the primary responsibility for their children. He cited a figure of 541,000 full-time dads that appeared in the *New York Times*, based on Census Bureau reports.

"But that's probably about half of what actually exists," Chris said. "I know in one area out here of 200 families, the Census Bureau found one full-time dad and projected that for the entire state. I think I'm the only one in the town where I live now, but in my old neighborhood in Minneapolis, I know there were a dozen in a ten-block radius. But how do you verify something like that?"

There wasn't much in Chris' background as a machinist to suggest he would find his niche as an at-home father.

"That decision actually came at a time when we were sure we'd never have children," he said. "We didn't have kids until we were in our thirties.

"Most of our friends had had children before then, and I just related to them better than my wife did. I'm more patient and laid-back; she's a Type-A personality. When the time came, we decided I was better suited than my wife to stay home with the kids."

He had one distinct problem right from the start.

"Parenting magazines," he said. "There'd always be that cover article on 'how to get your husband more involved.' I always had trouble relating to that."

Many full-time fathers say they have gotten both implicit and explicit messages that their efforts are not valued, and may even be unwelcome. Chris remembered another full-time dad from his Minneapolis neighborhood who took his daughter to a meeting of the local Brownies; the troop leader's husband called and told him not to come back.

"I know other men have run into that, but I've never had that kind of experience," Chris said. "There were a lot of people saying to me, 'We're watching you, we're going to see how [your kids] turn out, and if there's anything wrong, it's your fault.'

"But I always had a lot of people telling me how wonderful I was. I always volunteered to go on the field trips in my daughter's school, and she always thought it was neat that I got to know all her friends. And the teachers were always so happy to have a father along that I got to go on all the best trips."

But he suspects his daughter may have heard some disparaging comments about his unconventional fathering.

"I asked her once if anyone ever said anything about me, and she said 'No! And if they do, I don't care!'"

Chris thinks "there's no real way to determine the impact" he's had on his kids, and he wishes he had made a greater impact with the newsletter.

"As a rule, the full-time dad is pretty isolated," he said. "I was fortunate I had a friend, another guy doing the same thing with kids about the same age. It helps with the sleepless nights, the teething, to be able to call another guy and say, 'Hey, my kids are making me crazy!'

"That was another goal of *Full-Time Dads*, to help people find each other."

There is one gratification for Chris that can never be taken away: he tried.

"I'm taking the issues I published and putting them in plastic and keeping them safe, and my kids will always have them," he said. "Someday we're going to pass a newsstand and there's going to be a magazine there for full-time fathers, and my kids are going to know that their dad was ahead of his time."

On the Road Again

Buffalo, New York, 1976: Two parents, two jobs, one baby, one car.

When most fathers were on their way home to family and dinner at the end of a typical day, Jim Kelley was on his way to work at the Buffalo *News*, along with his baby daughter, Erin, ready to make the handoff to his wife, Susan, who was ending her day shift at the *News*.

Typical day:

"I'd be stuck in traffic, in the snow, on the (New York State) Thruway," Jim said, "driving with one hand, spooning out Beech-Nut baby food to my daughter with the other hand.

"I remember times I would walk into work at the paper with my briefcase under one arm and my kid in the car seat on the other. I'd put her down on my wife's desk, and my wife would take her back out and strap her into the car and head home—if she didn't get stuck for who knows how long in the snow."

Being in the forefront of the boom in two-career families meant the Kelleys were confronted by the child-care issue long before the array of choices available in the 1990s.

"We didn't want to just drop her in daycare. And at the time, it was extremely hard to find. Organized daycare was just getting started. We did go to one [center], and after a few days it was just terrible. It was like putting kids in pens. We decided we just couldn't do that. Our kid was coming home in tears."

Jim, now forty-two, travels in a men's world; he has covered the National Hockey League's Buffalo Sabres for a decade. But in those days, he learned about the isolation of being home with a baby, which was intensified by being a man in the predominantly woman's world of child care. He never encountered another man in a similar role. He learned to use the resource of a church-run cooperative program called "Mother's Day Out." He was always the only father bringing a child and volunteering his time.

"When I signed up," he said, "there were never any people who said, 'No, we don't want you,' but I'll tell you—it raised quite a few eyebrows because I was a man at home during the day raising my daughter."

But he achieved a unique status at potty time.

"The moms would just take the boys into the ladies' room and have them sit on the bowl," he said. "One day this one boy was tugging on my arm saying he had to go, so I took him in the men's room and he headed straight for the bowl. But I steered him the other way [to the urinal] and I said to him, 'Naw, you're a boy, this is how you do it.' I told him he could go home and tell his dad he knew how to 'go' like a man. I taught the other boys, and they were all crazy about it."

Erin, the Kelleys' first daughter, is now seventeen; with the long view of time, Jim appreciates the effect his early work on the second shift had on their relationship.

"I want to be careful in the way I say this, but the bond between my first daughter and myself is something special. A—because we did it and we survived, and B—because I learned so much about myself, about caring and about responsibility.

"It became really clear to me—more clear than from someone else telling me—just how much effect I would have on the shape and direction of Erin's life, on which way this child would go in her formative years. At times, that feeling was almost terrifying.

"I think when you have a child, it's your first focus on there being more to life than yourself. It takes you out of yourself, out of the 'me-first' attitude. You learn that other people matter, that what you do really can determine what they become."

The second shift is time that is invaluable, time that cannot be replaced.

"I wouldn't trade it for the world," Jim said. "I know I'm going to think about those times as long as I live."

Changing History
Joe Novotny had every reason to be a lousy father.

"When my mom saw me changing one diaper, she said, 'You already changed more diapers than your father ever did,'" Joe said. "My dad had seven boys and one girl. No wonder I felt such a void."

Worse than a lousy father, he might have become a dangerous one.

"I didn't remember a lot of things from my childhood," Joe

said. "But now I'm remembering a lot of stuff, a lot of past hurts, a lot of mental and physical abuse.

"My dad hit me a lot. He hit me often. Now my brothers hit their kids. My dad was abused by his dad. That's how it goes."

But that's not the way it turned out for him.

At night, Joe, thirty-four, drives a truck for the Illinois Department of Transportation. During the day on his second shift, he spends "every waking minute" with his two children, Becky, five, and Nick, three. His wife, Cheryl, has an office upstairs in their home on the North Side of Chicago. A former X-ray technician, Cheryl now has a business supplying Chicago-area hospitals with X-ray personnel. Their lives revolve around being close to their children.

"Parenting is my passion," Joe said. "I want to get the message out about how important it is."

Joe has a message and a mission. He runs a support group for fathers, which meets on the first Monday night of the month with the dads revolving as hosts; the meetings always start out with play-time with the host dad's children.

He has also coordinated parenting workshops and family workshops under the auspices of "Re-evaluation Counseling" (R.C.). In the context of parenting, the R.C. body of thought holds that a crying child needs to discharge her pain until it's gone; if we stop her from crying, the result is a buried hurt that will come back to haunt her again and again. If we allow a child to recover cleanly from her hurts when they happen, she won't have to deal with them later on.

"It's helped me tremendously, helped me to be a better parent," Joe said.

But he admits that, in his neighborhood, he is still marked as an unusual parent: a man who spends bountiful time with his kids.

"It's lonely," he said. "I don't have a lot of camaraderie with a lot of other dads. On our block, they look at me as a troublemaker. I know their wives are saying, 'Why aren't you out there in the front yard with your kids, instead of playing golf or watching a game?' or whatever else they're doing. I know they're all working guys, and they all put in a lot of hours on their jobs.

"But so do I."

He is on better terms with some of the mothers in the neighborhood, but not all of them.

"One woman watches my kids sometimes when I want to go for a run," said Joe, an accomplished distance runner. "But there's another woman who accused me of not having a penis. I guess that just showed her own level of distress."

What's most important is the reaction of his own children. He was startled and gratified by Becky's perceptiveness about his own growth as a parent.

"I must have told her that my dad hit me," Joe said, "I must have mentioned it somehow. Becky said, 'If your dad hit you as much as you say he did, how come you don't hit me? How come you don't hit us?'

"I couldn't believe she said that. I don't know how she made that association. But I told her that because I hated it when it was done to me, I knew I'd never do it."

Joe could have repeated history as a father; instead, he changed it. For his family, he created the kind of father he would have wanted for himself.

"I'm not exactly sure how it got started, or why," Joe said. "I just know that it's important. And I know it's fun."

The Father Notebook: How Many? How Much?

THERE IS NO MONEY in being a single mother. If you must be a single parent, be a single father.

Single-parent families headed by women of any racial group tend to have very thin cushions between themselves and the poverty level. Single-parent families headed by black women have virtually no cushion between themselves and the poverty level, which should come as no surprise to anyone who has been listening to what's been happening in America in the last twenty years.

But the fastest-growing segment of American family-group types—the single-parent families headed by fathers—have nearly double the median income of the corresponding family groups headed by mothers, in each racial category.

With a median income of $25,211, single fathers aren't exactly contacting their brokers by cellular phone from their Lexus sedans. But compared to single mothers, single fathers live on Easy Street, between High and Mighty. Their median income is almost double that of single mothers—a paltry $13,092.

New Traditions
The "traditional" American family, at least the one we remember from the old days of TV, no longer overwhelmingly dominates our population.

In 1970, the "married-couple" family (with or without children) comprised 70.5 percent of American households and 82.3 percent of the total population among households; by 1991, those figures had dropped to 55.3 percent of households and 68.5 percent of household population.

In 1970, married couples with children made up 40.3 percent of the total number of households; in 1991, they had dropped to 25.9 percent of total households.

In 1970, "other families" with children made up 5.0 percent of total households; in 1991, that share had grown to 8.5 percent. Father-child situations are the country's fastest-growing "other family type" (that's the Census Bureau description). In 1970, 90 percent of single-parent families were headed by mothers and only 10 percent by fathers. By 1991, that makeup had changed to 86 percent headed by mothers and 14 percent by fathers.

In 1991, according to census estimates, there were 1,365,000 family groups in the United States with children under eighteen that were headed by single fathers (broken down into four categories: divorced, widowed, never married, and "spouse absent"). That number had nearly doubled since 1980, when there were 690,000 family groups with children headed by fathers. The biggest increases were in the categories of "never married" fathers, from 63,000 family groups in 1980 to 285,000 family groups in 1991 (a whopping 350 percent increase); and divorced fathers, from 340,000 family groups in 1980 to 630,000 family groups in 1991 (an 85 percent increase).

Interestingly, the proportion of single-parent families headed by fathers is roughly equivalent among all races, according to 1991 census estimates.

Among all races, "father families" comprise 3.9 percent of the total of 34,973,000 family groups with children under eighteen.

Of 28,443,000 "white" family groups with children under eighteen, there were 1,068,000 father families (3.8 percent).

Of 5,173,000 "black" family groups with children under eighteen, there were 239,000 father families (4.6 percent).

Of 3,582,000 "Hispanic" family groups with children under eighteen, there were 158,000 father families (4.4 percent).

(To explain figures that don't add up, "Hispanics" may identify themselves as being of any race.)

How Many?

But how many at-home fathers are there? "An impossible statistic," said a researcher at the Chicago office of the Bureau of Labor Statistics, when asked about the number of two-parent families with children under eighteen where the mother works and the father is home as primary caregiver.

Let's try an extrapolation, anyway.

The Bureau of Labor Statistics actually does have a category of "men removed from the work force due to housekeeping responsibilities," with an estimate of about 250,000. But that doesn't tell us anything about family makeup (in fact, that description sounds more like a maid service than a family.)

Back to the Census Bureau. In the category of married-couple families, where both are considered to be "in the labor force" (working or seeking work), the data for March 1991 showed 653,000 couples with children under eighteen where only the wife was employed. Here again, we don't know if fathers were taking care of the kids or sitting in the den with the blinds closed, downing shooters and watching soaps. More seriously, there is no estimate on how many husbands were not in the labor force because they were disabled or unable to work for other reasons.

(By contrast, in this same category, the data showed 699,000 couples where only the husband was employed.)

Wait—there's another category, where only the wife is considered to be "in the labor force." The data showed 582,000 such couples (526,000 where the wife was employed, another 56,000 where the wife was unemployed).

So if we add up all the couples, we might estimate that somewhere between 1 million and 1.2 million married couples with children under eighteen are in a situation where the wife works and the husband is at home, with at least the opportunity to take on primary responsibility for child care.

Of course, there is absolutely no way to determine how many of those men cook dinner, too.

If we add that estimate of at-home fathers (1-1.2 million) to the number of single fathers (1.365 million), we have an estimate of somewhere around 2.5 million fathers who would appear to have the primary responsibility for child care in their family units.

Custody

One extremely significant arena where these changes in parenting are taking place is that of divorce custody. Jeff Atkinson, an attorney in Evanston, Illinois, and chairman of the American Bar Association's Child Custody Committee "off and on" over the last twelve years, says that in current divorce law, custody is no longer given automatically to the mother simply if she is "a fit mother."

The trend is toward equality in awarding custody, which is the theoretical basis of the law in forty-three states. There is moderate preference for mothers in the other seven states: In Florida, if all considerations are equal, the mother is preferred; the remaining six states consider the age and sex of children.

Atkinson takes surveys of the custody decisions reported in "courts of review" (i.e., supreme courts and courts of appeals). In a recent two-year period, 49 percent of the custody decisions went to the mother and 51 percent for father.

"These are not necessarily all contested cases," Atkinson said. "These are appellate cases, that don't just stop at trial level. And they're only the reported, or published, cases. Unpublished cases tend to be more usual in outcome. But we are definitely going toward a trend of equality."

Most of what will happen in the United States has probably already happened in California, including divorce and custody trends. California adopted a law in 1979 with an implied preference for joint custody, where children spend extended or roughly equal periods of time with each parent.

There are an average of 185,000 "family law" filings (concerning divorce, custody, property, finances) in California each year; only 5 to 10 percent actually go before a judge, according to James Cook of the Joint Custody Association in Los Angeles.

According to Cook's figures, 66 percent of divorcing parents in California decide voluntarily on joint custody, which is determined by the timing that is best for the child, adapting to the natural breaks in the child's schedule (primarily for schooling).

"People usually start out pressing very hard for absolutely equal time," Cook said. "When you tell them they don't have to fight for it, that they're going to get joint custody, and you ask them how much time they actually have to give—well, sometimes things do change a little."

What About the Children?
What has increased father involvement meant for children? How are children affected by growing up with a single-parent father or strongly involved father?

"A lot of research backs up the fact that children do quite well," said Dr. Brad Sachs, a psychologist and founder of The Father

Center in Columbia, Maryland. "Research has shown that the more saliently involved a father is, the children have better self-confidence, a better sense of social mastery, they are more flexible in gender identification and they do less stereotyping. And I've seen that in my own experience."

Dr. Kyle Pruett, of the Yale University Child Study Center, has been conducting a long-term study of seventeen two-parent families in the New England area, in which the fathers started out as primary caregivers for the children—in essence, "at-home fathers." Pruett says his study has found no significant differences between these children and other children, except in their identification of the father as a "maker" of life along with the mother. He also says he has found no significant differences between the fathers who retained the role of primary caregiver and those who relinquished that role over time.

In *The Nurturing Father* (Warner Books, 1987), Pruett summed up: "It seems that efforts to find some special predictor, quality, experience or portent that sets these men and their kin apart from the rest of us are so far unsuccessful. Would it not be a most profound finding for these men NOT to be so different from the rest of their species in substance or experience?"

The Diaper Diary

Diaper Diary

Does it take a macho man to change a diaper?

That question surprised me, even if it was asked with a smile. I always accepted diaper-changing as part of the parenting deal, like mucking out the stable if you want your own horse.

After six months, averaging ten changes a day, Jenny went through about 1,800 diaper changes. I probably handled 1,000 of them. We faced our only crisis when Jenny was about two months old: she pooped thirteen times in one day. She was fine in every other way, and our pediatrician said not to worry, so we kept changing diapers (it was the only time I remember hoping it was Joan's turn). But we survived, and Jenny thrived.

We never had another day like that one, though not all the diaper changes were simple or routine. Jenny sprayed me and oozed onto me many times. Once she even opened up all the valves while she was in my arms—without a diaper. Call it my daddy initiation. She was a baby, and that's what babies do. Cleaning up simply came with the job.

Not all men felt this way, I learned. One friend confessed he was so overwhelmed by one bowel blast, he was ready to take his son out on the lawn to use the garden hose on him. So I guess the macho threshold depends on the man.

But it also may depend on the diaper.

We used old-fashioned cotton diapers, from a trusty, old-fashioned diaper service. We held them together with water-resistant cotton diaper covers equipped with that modern miracle, Velcro. We wanted cotton next to Jenny's skin because it was light, cool, and breathable, and because it wasn't made of materials we couldn't understand, pronounce, or trust.

Cotton diapers are not as convenient as disposables. They leak. Diaper covers, and often clothes, get wet and dirty. So they create a bit more laundry than disposables do, adding to the burden if you don't happen to have a washer and dryer in your home. And if you're away from your diaper pail, you have to store them until you return.

Still, having soft cotton next to Jenny's bottom gave us a feeling of satisfaction. But we have three confessions to make.

First: we did use disposable diapers for several months when we were doing any kind of traveling, though we painstakingly sought out chemical-free, biodegradable disposables. Using cloth diapers when you're traveling can make you crazy.

Second: Joan, Jenny, and I have contributed to spoiling the environment. For most of Jenny's first two months, we used the same big-name, disposable, chemical-filled, nonbiodegradable diapers everyone else uses. So two months' worth of Jenny's diapers will be around for 100 years in some landfill.

Third: what changed our minds about disposables was not consideration of the earth's environment, but of Jenny's personal environment.

The paper in most disposable diapers has been treated with chlorine bleach to make it white. The bleaching process on wood pulp produces dioxin, a possible carcinogen which no one seems to want in coffee filters any more. Gold coffee filters appeared in a hurry when dioxin was fingered by the media, but where were the gold diapers?

Most disposables use acrylic acid polymer salts to absorb moisture. Acrylic acid, which in certain forms is a highly corrosive liquid, was one of the original substances used to make plastic.

The polymer salts wick away moisture and in the process turn into a gel, which sits next to a baby's skin, becoming heavier and more solid with time. If the gel becomes wet enough, it will eventually turn into a solid plastic. The environmental question on disposables has focused on the plastic backing being nonbiodegradable, but the plastic formed inside the diaper may be just as indestructible. And since the inside surface feels dry, chemical-laden diapers tend to stay on a baby longer. So any urea or fecal matter that is not absorbed by the diaper will stay in contact with baby's skin longer.

We decided we would not deliberately expose Jenny to any chemical risks, no matter how slight, just for our own convenience. We didn't want her bottom sheathed in solid, nonbreathing plastic all day and night. We didn't want dioxins next to her skin. Once our consciousness was raised, we switched immediately to the cotton diapers—and eventually, we cut out disposables altogether, even when we were traveling. We found that diaper services all over the country are willing and able to get diapers to you just about any place and any time you need them.

Sure, cotton diapers involved a little more work and attention than the disposables. But there was more air reaching Jenny's skin, and skin must breathe. And once we switched to cotton diapers, Jenny was virtually free of diaper rash. We never used powders or creams. We simply changed her often, and let her little bottom "air dry" before putting on another diaper.

Using cotton diapers meant we did a little more laundry, and sometimes it meant that our hands got dirty. But we came to feel that the environment touching Jenny was inseparable from the environment touching everyone else. The extra work felt worthwhile. And if my hands got dirty, that just showed I was doing my job.

The Future

WILL JENNY STILL NEED ME WHEN I'M SIXTY-FOUR?
She'll be a young woman then, a couple of years out of college (we hope), and probably well off on her life's adventure. If she's like Joan and I were at that stage, she probably won't be calling or visiting as often as we would like. Well, she'd better call—even if it's collect.

What an overbearing father. Jenny was six months old, she couldn't yet say the word "Hello," and there I was, already worrying about her saying "Goodbye."

You bet I was worried about it. Because I had seen the future, and it hurt.

The future came to me in a Disney animated movie, *The Little Mermaid*, which should be rated "ND"—No Dads with Daughters. Actually, it's a nice little story until the climax. The little mermaid has fallen in love with a human. She herself must become human, and never return to her home under the sea, or else give up the man she loves.

In a cruel twist of plot, the decision is left to her father, the king of the sea. He decides, as a good father must, that his daughter shall have the freedom to lead her own life. So he points his trident-scepter and begins the magical transformation, knowing his daughter never will return to him.

"No! No!" I wanted to shout. "Don't let her go! Not for him! Not for that simp! He's not good enough for her! No! No!"

Stupid cartoon. I walked around the rest of the day with a lump in my throat. Still get one, whenever I think about that goodbye scene and what it portends. My little Jenny, going away some day? Not my little girl! But of course I will have to face the fact of her going away, some day.

Would I feel as sad over a son's leaving? I had to admit I probably would not. I know I would have loved a son as deeply as I've loved Jenny, and I would have treated him as gently and kindly as I've treated her. I know it isn't fair to have a double standard of expectations. But if I'm honest, I also know there is a difference. My role may not be that of a traditional father, but at heart I guess I'm a throwback. Jenny is my little sweetheart.

At least I found I wasn't alone in feeling that way. My brother-in-law, whose daughter was four years old at the time, said *The Little Mermaid* made him as miserable as it made me. But I was lucky: I only saw the video once, and it was at his house. His daughter played it over and over. She loved it. He just had to endure it.

But knowing about the pain that lies ahead may help us cope when it arrives. We will have countless little goodbyes along the way to prepare us.

We've already said goodbye to the infant who could curl into a ball, practically fitting into the palm of my hand. We'll say goodbye to the baby who is all-dependent, as she becomes a child beginning to test her independence.

We'll say goodbye to the child who has always been under foot at home as she goes to school for the first time. We'll say goodbye to our little pal as she becomes an adolescent, wanting to spend all her time with her friends. We'll say goodbye to the high-school girl going off to college, her first real life without us—and begin our life without her.

And an older parent can't help thinking about that longest goodbye. We can't ignore reality, meaning mortality; we must plan for it. So Joan and I began working on our wills. (You mean I'm actually going to die? Ugh.) We've already begun a financial plan for Jenny's education. If she has the ability and determination, we don't want her to lack the resources.

Yet there is far more life to our future than planning for farewells. We see the future in the faces of little girls out walking with their parents: a two-year-old intently holding onto a doll, a five-year-old scampering about at the zoo, a ten-year-old seriously choosing clothes. Joan and I smile at each other and say: "We'll have a Jenny like that before long." Already, we'd met a new Jenny who laughed, who picked up a rattle, who wanted to walk, who grew two front teeth. We found more love, more joy, more wonder each day.

There aren't many years before I'm sixty-four, and I know the time will pass too quickly. When I thought about becoming a father at forty, I was frightened of being attached to a child into my sixties. Now I feel privileged.

Wondering

Your eyes were big, blue questions, Jenny. What was going on behind them in those first six months? Without words, how could you fill your days with thoughts?

But you didn't need words to express yourself. A day-long song was on your lips, streaming unchecked and unfiltered from your emotions. If we didn't understand what you were saying, we often could tell what you were feeling. And even without thoughts or words as we know them, you had the boundless curiosity of a scientist or explorer.

You were on a mission from the moment of birth, a mission to know everything and everyone around you. You would study things, look into them, puzzle over them. You wanted to understand them, and you would focus on them until you did understand them—or until you were thwarted by frustration. We knew you'd try again before long. You always did.

How were you able to learn so quickly? You were about five months old when I was holding you upright in your crib one day. You were swiping at the figures in your mobile, upset when you couldn't catch one in your left hand. So I showed you how to reach out with both hands, trapping one of those bouncing cartoon characters between them. You succeeded after two or three tries. After that lesson, you always reached out with both hands to make your catch, like an old-fashioned outfielder.

When you were six months old, we were out back in the garden and I showed you how to work the latch on the gate. A few days later, we tried it again. This time, you reached out and grasped the handle, and pushed on the latch until you opened it. Was it just something there to be pushed? Or had you actually figured out how it worked by watching me do it?

You always watched us so closely. Was that the way you learned to eat with a spoon? Your mom and I were startled when we began giving you cereal at six months: you grabbed the spoon and steered it to your mouth! You held onto it and put it back into your mouth to get more of the cereal.

Then you began to help us with each feeding. Your hands and face were layered with cereal, squash, or sweet potato, but we tried not to discourage you. Why shouldn't you help feed yourself, if you were ready and eager to do it?

Eager: now there's a word to describe you. Always eager to move, to move on, to reach the next place or next stage. You never wanted to be held back from your experiments with life, especially by something as unproductively stationary as a nap. You could nearly sit up on your own at this point, but sitting still was another matter. If we tried to get you to sit on the floor, you would often begin straining to stand up. "Let's get going!" you seemed to be saying.

In *The Magic Years*, a premier work on child psychology, Selma Fraiberg portrayed a baby who was just like you: "This urge for discovery is like an insatiable hunger that drives him on relentlessly. He is drunk with fatigue, but he cannot stop. The hunger for sensory experience is as intense and all-consuming as the belly-hunger of the first months of life . . . this indefatigable globetrotter makes it very clear that he is not interested in any naps, thank you, he just has too much work to do."

But she was writing about a child who was nearly a year old, Jenny. You had us worn out in half that time. We wondered (in fact, we worried): what would you be like when you were a year old? Would we be able to keep up? Your fortysomething parents often feared we wouldn't make it through your first year.

Your first six months were so hard, for you and for us. You cried so much, and with such anguish. Even after those dispiriting times had passed, you could still cry, dramatically, spectacularly. Even craftily, I sometimes suspected. But then you would laugh, and anyone who could hear you or see you was yours for the taking.

When we gave you a ride in a playground swing, your yelps and squeals could take anyone's heart to the sky. They had just that effect on our friend Mel Boruszak. He was with us on your first playground visit; in fact, he gave you your first official swing ride. He was eighty-eight and you were about five months old, and it was hard to tell who was having a better time. "I've never seen anything like it!" he kept saying. You knew you were alive, and you were delighted. So was everyone around you.

How much did you know about us, the two people who were carrying you around, feeding you, changing you, making funny faces and noises at you, and trying to get you to go to sleep?

The experts like Fraiberg said you wouldn't be able to differentiate our faces, or know who we were, until you were at least eight months old. Then why did your face light up when you saw us? Why did you whimper when I left to wash my hands while I was changing you? Why did you cry when your mom left for work? And if you didn't recognize our faces, why did you smile at our wedding picture?

We always wondered about you, Jenny, as you were wondering about the world around you. What was going on behind those inquisitive eyes? In your own time, we knew, you would tell us.

Kitchen Conquest

(When we last left our hero in the kitchen in July 1989, his cooking future looked dark and grim. Could the at-home father adjust to preparing real food in a real kitchen for a real family? Could he overcome the patterns of half a lifetime: eating out and dialing room service? We return after the passage of twelve months.)

Dad is the name. Meat loaf is the game.

A year later, nothing was the same. The kitchen was no threat to me. I no longer needed a baseball bat for self-defense in there. Breakfast, lunch, or dinner; inside on the stove or outside on the grill, you name the meal and I could do it.

Within reason, of course.

My specialties: meat loaf, fish, and barbecued chicken. I even made a name for myself with one meal, grilled swordfish steaks, that a friend of ours insisted on calling the best fish he'd ever had. It's too bad Jenny wasn't ready to sample any of my specialties yet; at seven months old, she had to wait a while.

I even had my own apron, a blue denim workshop-style, from Halles-Villette (whatever that is) in Paris. It made me look and feel official, and feeling official in the kitchen was half the battle.

The other half was knowing how to read.

That's what Joan, a wonderful cook, kept telling me while trying to help me overcome my trepidation over food preparation: "If you can read, you can cook." Sure, but who wanted to read that stuff in the first place?

In fact, some of our early attempts at "team cooking" only reinforced my bias against the kitchen in general, and cooks who wrote cookbooks in particular. One experience, in the autumn of 1989 while Joan was pregnant, almost kept me out of the kitchen permanently.

We were cooking with a friend at his condo, putting together a big dinner with more friends coming over later. The recipe, for something that looked like moss-covered chicken, came from a cookbook that I think was titled *The Condescending Gourmet*. It took more than three hours of one tedious step after another. I spent the last hour of the preparation looking at the lake view from the living-room window, with a beer in one hand and my head in the other.

Aside from the outlandish amount of time it took, the recipe had another major turn-off for me: it called for saffron. If you buy saffron off the spice shelf in a supermarket, you pay about nine dollars and you get a half-teaspoon of the stuff. To me, that wasn't cooking: that was snobbish nonsense.

Keep reading, Joan encouraged me. Eventually, in that same cookbook, I came upon a quick, simple recipe for broiled fish with an orange-tomato sauce. I tried it, and it was delightful.

If I could cook something with that fine a taste, maybe cooking wasn't such a menial chore after all. Joan kept telling me that my major problem was not having a base of knowledge or experience, and that once I made a few meals, I would gain confidence.

Confidence isn't automatic. It comes from surviving experiences like the fish filet that insisted on moving after it was cooked, trying to slide down into the back of the broiler. I got so aggravated, I bounced a spatula off the floor (great shot, too: I broke the spatula). I also body-slammed a frying pan after another disaster.

But I knew things were changing by New Year's morning of 1990, when I held three-week-old Jenny in my left arm and made Joan's breakfast with my right. Joan was too exhausted to get out of bed. The breakfast was only fried eggs, sausage, toast, juice, and coffee, but I got the cooking order right so that everything finished at (approximately) the same time. And I added my own flourish: I cracked the eggs cleanly on the side of the frying pan, without breaking the yolks—and I did it with one hand. (I picked up this technique from watching that galloping gourmet, Clint Eastwood, in *For a Few Dollars More.*)

My experiences with Jenny helped me along the way. Once you've handled a baby and changed diapers, getting your hands messy in the kitchen isn't such a big deal. I was no longer turned off by plunging my hands up to the elbows into a bowl of mushy ground beef, milk, eggs, cracker crumbs, and secret ingredients; it's the only way to make meat loaf. I even overcame my horror of handling raw chicken, which I had always thought was the slimiest, grossest stuff around.

Joan left to me the more intricate workings of the microwave oven, figuring I was better prepared to understand it because of my engineering studies in college twenty years earlier. But Joan remained in charge of the steaming, food-milling, and pureeing of the fresh fruits and vegetables we used for Jenny's first solid foods. (After reading this far, did you really expect us to do something the easy way?) She was still the one with that certain touch, that certain sense, that certain—*je ne sais quoi*. (See? I really did read some cook books!)

But I knew my day would come. I couldn't wait for Jenny to taste my meat loaf.

The Babysitter

WHEN SHE WAS SIX MONTHS OLD, JENNY FOUND A NEW PAL.
Meg, a high-school student who lived in our neighborhood, began coming to our house each afternoon to take care of Jenny. But calling her a babysitter wouldn't do her justice. She was Jenny's first pal.

Joan always knew it would make sense to have help in caring for Jenny. I always said no: a stranger in our house, with our child? Why was I staying home, if not to take care of Jenny?

"But you know it will help to get a break," Joan would say. "You need a break sometimes."

I usually answered her perceptive suggestion with an equally perceptive comment, such as: "Don't tell me what I need!"

The question of help was a land mine for me. I felt I needed to prove I could do it on my own, that I could take care of Jenny, keep the house running, and get my own work done, without any help. I had set out to do it this way, and no one was going to tell me I couldn't.

So I did it my own way—alone. Jenny and I were together all day from Monday through Friday. If I needed time to run an errand or do some work, I would try to jam it into the hour or so that Joan was home for lunch.

The days got longer. One rainy day I ran the gamut of morning activities, from songs through stories, then looked at the clock: 8:39 A.M. Hey, less than four hours until Joan was home for lunch!

Tempers got shorter. Jenny seemed especially obstreperous one long afternoon, playing around when I was trying to feed her breast milk in a cup. I lost my patience and pulled her hands off the cup handles, ready to force her to take the milk. Jenny looked up at me, first startled, then wounded, and began crying. I felt like a rotten dad. I was waiting for the Baby Police to crash through the door and haul me away in handcuffs.

I decided Joan was right.

We hired Meg early in June of Jenny's first year. Meg sounded self-assured over the telephone, and she was poised when she came to our house to be interviewed. She told us her toughest babysitting job had been caring for five children at once. She was gentle and friendly with Jenny from the first time she held her and spoke to her. We felt there wasn't any decision for us to make: Meg had made it for us.

The first few days were difficult. Jenny was unsure of what to make of this new person, and I was more nervous than Jenny. I hovered. If Jenny cried more than a few seconds, I was right on the scene. Fortunately, Meg was patient with Jenny and even more patient with me.

Meg and Jenny would never develop a rapport if I kept jumping in, so I forced myself to sit at my desk. And I realized I wasn't simply concerned for Jenny's well-being: I was jealous. I was jealous of someone else spending so much time with Jenny, and possibly taking care of her as well as I could. I was jealous of Jenny being happy with someone else. It was a humbling self-discovery.

It takes a leap of faith to entrust your child to someone else's hands, but I soon had to admit that Meg was doing an excellent job. She was completely involved, and thoroughly confident—and extremely competent. She read to Jenny, played with her, took her on walks, took her to the playground, even got her to nap occasionally. She quickly noticed what Jenny liked and didn't like. We quickly noticed how much Jenny liked her.

With time for my own work and chores, I got along more easily with Jenny. We laughed more. Instead of feeling burned out at the end of the day, I was eager to be with her again. If Joan was tired out after a day's work, I wasn't resentful that she couldn't just take over with Jenny; I had enough energy left to take up the slack.

As much as Meg helped us (especially me), she gave Jenny an invaluable lesson in learning how to relate to other people, how to depend on them, and how to like them. Jenny will always feel Meg's influence, even if she doesn't remember Meg.

Jenny will need other people all through her life, and part of my job as a parent is to help her meet the people she needs: I can't be her only pal. Working at my desk in the afternoon, I would sometimes eavesdrop on happy sounds coming from another part of the house, and I knew we had done what was best for Jenny.

Everybody needs a pal.

The Fathercize Program

A BABY DOESN'T HAVE TO WEIGH YOU DOWN.

When Jenny came along, Joan and I discovered what many new parents have learned: it's easy to get most of your exercise going to and from the refrigerator. We used to get away from pressure with a few laps around the track at the health club; now, if we got a break, we were more likely to head straight for the Haagen-Dazs.

But a parent doesn't have to turn into a blob. I devised a fitness program to provide me with vigorous exercise right in the home, without costly equipment or exorbitant health club fees. Here is "Fathercize," the Ten-Point At-Home Father's Fitness Program:

1. Instant Shower: Get those muscles warm and loose to start the day by showering at a fast and furious pace, with a goal of being in and out during a five-minute radio news broadcast. That's about all the time you'll have, anyway.

2. Rug Gliding: Your baby likes trying to walk to get her day going? Great! Take advantage. Bending over and holding her upright by her hands, slide backwards along the rug on your knees as she walks. Turn around and repeat. Great for the knees, hips, and especially the lower back. Knee pads are optional.

3. Stairway Sprints: A key exercise. With your baby in the crib about to be changed, in the high chair about to be fed, or in the stroller about to go outdoors, sprint up the stairs for something you've forgotten. Get back before the baby cries. I used the Townhouse Tour variation: with Jenny on the second floor, I would sprint to retrieve something on the third floor, discover that it was actually on the first floor, fly downstairs, and then bound back up to the second floor. I never quite completed the circuit before she started to cry, but that's the brass ring. (Note: wimps who live in condos must substitute an exercise of suitable difficulty.)

4. Overhead Hoist: Grasping the baby under the armpits, lift her straight up into the air until your arms are fully extended. Lower her until you can kiss her nose. Repeat several times. Great for the shoulders, biceps, and back, with the weight increasing each day.

5. Power Strolling: While pushing the baby in a stroller, walk with sufficient speed and purpose to convince witnesses you actually have somewhere to go. Vary your route on each lap around the neighborhood, to avoid amused whispers of "There he is again!"

6. Heavy Walking: Similar to Power Strolling, but the baby is strapped to your chest in a front-carrier. Excellent cardiovascular conditioner. Fathers who are expert at Heavy Walking are permitted to feel smug when overhearing a mother declare: "I carried this baby for nine months, now it's your turn!"

7. Marathon Carry: A specialty with babies who won't nap unless they're in Dad's arms, and wake up as soon as they sense they're being lowered to a flat surface. With the baby in your arms, continue walking through an entire nap. My record is 102 minutes (with an asterisk: I got through the last twenty-one minutes because Joan brought me a beer).

8. Telephone Dive: You have just put your baby to sleep when the telephone rings. From a standing start, dive to the telephone and answer it before it rings a second time. Also effective with a doorbell. Automatic disqualification from the program if you attempt the dive with the baby in your arms.

9. High-speed Housework: As wife and baby fall asleep at night, quietly go downstairs and begin cleaning up. Quickly increase pace, striving to raise pulse rate over 100. Use music in headphones at high volume to set the tempo. My own choice was the Rolling Stones' *Hot Rocks*. I found a nice irony in taking out the garbage while Mick Jagger was pleading, "I can't get no satisfaction," or in cleaning up the dishes while he satirized "Mother's Little Helper."

10. Twelve-ounce Curl: This exercise ties the whole program together. After completing the High-speed Housework, go to the refrigerator for a cold bottle of electrolyte-replenishing fluid (my favorite has a black label, made by Miller). Open it. With your elbow on a flat surface, raise the bottle to your lips. Repeat. Repeat. Repeat.

The program works. In seven months, my weight dropped from 177 pounds to 172 pounds, and I've maintained it near that point. The weight-loss curve did flatten out, but that's only to be expected: I weighed 195 pounds when I met Joan in 1986, and 188 pounds when we were married in 1987. Marriage and a family can work wonders on a body.

The results might have been more dramatic if I had dropped Exercise Ten from the program. But I decided that body shape doesn't matter if the soul isn't kept fit, too.

The Screamer

Jenny was about seven months old when she began screaming.

"What will we do," Joan wondered one night, "if someone hears her and calls the police?"

If the police just looked at Jenny (with their ears plugged, of course), they would see a happy baby with a face-filling smile. But if they unplugged their ears at the right (or wrong) moment, they might think murder was being committed, or at least a purse-snatching.

Even Meg, our babysitter, had to arm herself against public reaction when she and Jenny were outdoors.

"Sometimes she screams when I have her in the carriage," Meg said, "and people turn around and look, like they're thinking: 'What are you doing to that child? Is she tied up?'"

No, Jenny was not tied up. But she was wrapped up in learning how alive she is. It's as if she understood that she was really making her own noises, and she wanted to test the limits: "How loud can I get? How long can I hold it?"

"EEE-EEEEEEEEEE-EEEK!"

She didn't break any glass, but we kept a constant eye on the crystalware. Would she get much louder as she grew? We feared for our mirrors, even our windows.

Sometimes we could spot Jenny winding up for a scream. She took a deep breath, hunched up her shoulders, opened her mouth as wide as possible, positioned her tongue, and let fly. Her eyes would narrow in concentration. Her tongue would quiver. The pitch was so high, neither Joan nor I could reproduce it; Jenny seemed to be pushing against the upper limit of the human auditory range. We couldn't stop it—not that we would ever want to stifle her. All we could do was try not to mind when we felt it drilling into our ears.

Or when we felt people's eyes boring into us.

We were at a little coffee shop in our neighborhood one evening when Jenny got a little restless and I took her outside for some fresh air. She'd become fascinated by bicycles, and it was just our luck that a little boy came pedaling past us.

Uh-oh. Jenny saw the bike and wound up.

"AHHH-EEEEEEEEEE-EEE! YOW!"

A woman getting out of her car was startled and nearly tripped over the curb. "Oh, my God!" she said, "What—" and then she turned and saw it was Jenny. "Oh, it's a *baby*!" she said, regaining her balance but remaining incredulous.

Meanwhile, Jenny had the excited look on her face that accompanied all her outbursts, as if she were thinking: "Wow! Did I do that? Hey, that's great! That was ME!"

Jenny's screaming was another factor to consider in our constant search for places we could go with a baby. No outing was simple, not even for breakfast on a Saturday morning.

Jenny's near-constant crying made eating out—or most other trips—nearly unthinkable for most of her first six months. In rare quiet moments, Joan and I fantasized about restaurants we had known and loved, and wondered if we would ever see them again.

When Jenny became calmer and more in tune with her surroundings, we began to look around for restaurants that welcomed children. Dinner destinations were practically nonexistent; lunch spots generally were too busy. Breakfast was the best bet; once summer rolled around, breakfast places with outdoor spaces were ideal. Whenever we could, we went out to breakfast on the weekends.

We survived a few episodes of crying. We survived two huge bowel blasts, the first by rushing through breakfast and heading home, the second by changing her right in the booth. We even survived the faulty recommendation of a North Side bistro as being "great for kids;" the kids, it turned out, were the twenty-year-old variety who seemed uncertain of where babies came from, but quite certain they didn't want them around.

When we survived those challenges, we thought we could coast for a while. We had forgotten that when you think you have things figured out with a baby, it just means everything is going to change. The screaming was one of those changes.

Out of desperation, we adopted a strategy: if we saw Jenny winding up in a public place, with no quick exit, we made sure people could see us laughing. We made sure our hands were in plain sight, above the table. We made sure we said things like, "Hey, that's really fun, isn't it? You're just having a great time!"

No one ever called the police, but we certainly scared the cool out of some people. We would have scared a lot more of them if they had been around at bath-time. Jenny always loved her bath. And you know what that means.

Crawling Together

JENNY AND I LEARNED ABOUT CRAWLING TOGETHER. Life was a lot different down on the floor.

There are all sorts of discoveries to be made at the eye level of a crawling baby: a penny, a clump of dirt that was missed by the vacuum cleaner, a staple that popped up through the carpet, a crust of bread dating from the late eighties, and one of those sinister little plastic fasteners that has to be removed from every piece of clothing and every toy manufactured today.

Every one of those discoveries could be a hazard. So the at-home father got down on his hands and knees, exploring the floor and picking at the rug.

I found constant threats, constant rebukes. Look at those plugs and electrical outlets: why haven't you covered them? And that expandable coffee table: look at those treacherous metal hinges and edges underneath! Replace it with something simple, with rounded edges. The kitchen: latch those cabinets closed!

How many more dangers? Keep crawling, and find them.

But all was not work down at floor level. Jenny and I read books, we played games, we laughed, and we had crawling lessons, with demonstrations by Dad and by various stuffed animals.

Most of Jenny's early crawling pushed her backwards, and she had to learn to get her knees up under her belly and rock forward. Sometimes she would just bounce down on her face, but sometimes she'd get a hand out and inch herself forward. Then, a big smile and a little shriek: "Look what I did!" But Jenny also got frustrated when she became stuck in one place and couldn't move forward. I often felt the same way.

I had never spent so much time in one place. For some twenty-five years, from entering high school until quitting my sportswriting job, I spent little time at home—any home.

Even after moving to Chicago, I never really unpacked my bags. My work had me hopping around North America for nine months of the year, and in the summer I traveled: England, Mexico, Alaska, Japan, China. In our first two years of marriage, Joan and I probably spent a year together and a year apart, considering the traveling I did for my job.

Then I became an at-home father, whose world was as wide as a walk around the neighborhood. I sighed when an airplane flew overhead. I mused over those summer journeys. My favorite old leather carry-on bag became Jenny's diaper bag.

Joan understood how stuck I could feel. "You need to get out more," she would say. "Do something for yourself and bring Jenny along." That usually meant driving. Flying never bothered me much. But behind the wheel with Jenny strapped into her car seat, I became an amalgamation of jitters. I knew I would only be safe in one car: a resurrected 1965 Pontiac. (Remember that chrome battering ram on the front end?)

Yet I knew Joan was right. And I had to pick myself up off the floor on a day when Joan had early-morning meetings and our babysitter could not work that afternoon.

That morning, I collected myself for a drive to the North Side, alone with Jenny, to visit Joan's mom and walk to the Lincoln Park Zoo. Jenny curiously watched an elephant head-butting a tree, a sea lion basking on a rock in the sun, and a rhino standing around, looking bored.

The trip home went smoothly, and I dared to plan a real adventure for the afternoon: a subway ride with Jenny to a bookstore in the South Loop.

My knees were shaky as I descended the steps to the subway platform, but Jenny fell asleep in her front pouch, her head leaning trustfully against my chest. She didn't even awaken as the train thundered into the station. She never slept through the night—how could she sleep through that racket?

Awakening as we got to the store, Jenny looked around at the books, the colors, the lights, and the woman working at the desk. We found three posters for Jenny's room: one was an illustration from *Good Night, Moon*, one of her favorite books, and she loved it. And we found paperback reprints of some favorite old books of mine, memories from my own childhood. As we wandered among the shelves, Jenny would sometimes tilt her head back and look up at me, and when I met her eyes she would smile as if to say: "This is neat, Dad!"

That day was one of our best ever. We hadn't gone far, but Jenny and I had become traveling companions. Even traveling at a crawl, our little journeys could add up to big discoveries.

And back home, back down on the floor, Jenny did something new: she crawled up over my leg and slid down the other side, with a smile and a little shriek as she came to a stop.

A small world takes as much exploring as a big one.

Fight Games

AFTER JENNY WAS BORN, Joan and I had to learn to talk all over again.

But not to Jenny. To each other.

In the first months, our conversations often were limited to a litany of questions and answers focused on Jenny: Did she sleep? Eat? Wet? Poop? Are her clothes washed? Were the diapers delivered? Only then could we get to important personal matters: Do we have anything for dinner (or breakfast, or lunch)? Can you hold her for a while?

"I used to wonder about those surveys that said married couples talk to each other about twenty minutes a week," Joan said. "Now I'm starting to understand how that can happen."

With communication goes intimacy, and physical intimacy is not even the most important kind (though it's certainly not to be underestimated). We began missing those little impromptu conversations where we'd tell each other how we were feeling, what we were thinking, what we were anticipating, what we were dreading, what was fun and what was difficult.

Those little talks are the marks of real intimacy, and parenting can squeeze them out of the picture. We didn't realize it, but squeezing out those little intimacies meant we were heading for confrontations.

What creates a confrontation? My friend John Madden, the psychologist, had a favorite saying: "What seems to be bothering you usually isn't what's *really* bothering you."

I seldom recognize it at the time, but when I'm ready to scrap, it's usually because I'm fighting against myself. Often it's because the three "T-factors" are out of control: Time, Tension, and Tiredness.

There never seems to be enough time to do all the things you need to do—or even half of them. You feel tension over trying to meet your child's needs, your partner's needs, and your own needs. You're always tired, and fatigue can do a nasty job on your feelings.

The three "T's" add up to a fourth "T:" Trouble, with your partner a likely target.

The easiest course to take is to shut down, act out your misery, and try to make everyone else feel as rotten as you do. The most difficult course is to try to understand what's going on inside yourself, and why you're feeling so ugly. Guess which course is best? Nobody said this was going to be easy.

Simply saying, "Boy, do I feel crummy!" can open the lines of communication when things are going badly. If your partner is able to listen without feeling blamed or threatened, you've found yourself a great partner, and you're well on your way to solving your problem.

Just saying you feel crummy can take a lot of self-awareness and courage. But it can be the beginning of owning up to your feelings, being honest about them and being able to say "I feel angry" instead of "You make me mad!"

At that level of honesty, acting on your feelings becomes a choice, not a compulsion. You can be in control. You may be able to solve a problem without swinging at someone. The process can take years; unfortunately, most of us don't have that much time.

So when self-awareness eludes us, we fight. There's nothing wrong with fighting, as long as you fight by some rules.

Joan and I try to stick to the matter at hand, without opening a file cabinet of grievances; we don't call names; we don't use or threaten physical confrontations; and we don't throw "the kitchen sink," the emotional weapon to end all weapons.

The rules work—except when they don't. We've had some first-class blowups since beginning to cope with parenthood. After one of our differences of opinion, Joan left for work with a frosty farewell and I went way too far with a wounding response.

Even during the confrontation, I was aware of operating on at least three levels: on the most accessible level, I was determined to play out this little show of anger, as dramatically as I could; on a level that seemed somehow detached, I told myself I sounded really silly; and on a level directly connected to my heart, I regretted my words as soon as I said them.

Later, we talked and held to the rules, though it was no strain by then. We had blown our tops and relieved some pressure. Our little bout had cleared the air, we felt better, and we were talking again.

We've always taken the risk of talking again, and it has always paid off. Blowups are never easy and never enjoyable, but they can serve a purpose. No rules are as important as the desire to keep trying to make things right.

In fact, I don't think you need any specific rules, except these three: be kind, be generous, be forgiving. I can't act that way all the time; I suspect no one can, without a halo. But you get points for trying. A lot of points.

The Skin of Her Teeth

JENNY WAS RUBBING HER GUMS furiously with her little fist, scrunching up her face and making painful noises.

Teething, right? But she wasn't even four months old. Could she possibly be teething?

"No, no teeth there," said the doctor. "Much too early for teeth to be coming in."

"Nothing coming through," said the dentist. "Too early."

Searching for answers, Joan and I took Jenny to our highest authority: Joan's mom, who raised seven children through nearly 350 teeth, in their first and second sets.

"She's definitely teething," said Catherine.

Medically, teething means teeth are beginning to emerge. But practically, as Joan's mom well knew, teething means a long, painful process before the first white enamel sprouts from a swollen gum. Just remember your last toothache. This is far worse.

"If adults ever experienced the kind of pain a baby feels in teething, they would pass out," our dentist said.

How do we cope, short of unconsciousness? There is no shortage of recommended remedies: anesthetic gel; ice; whiskey, with or without water, applied to the gums; teething rings; biting on a spoon; biting on the hard heel of a loaf of Italian bread; frozen cubes of apple juice; chewing on a damp washcloth; hard pretzels; teething biscuits; doorknobs; parents' fingers (parents may then need whiskey); massaging the gums; biting the edges of tables, chairs, cribs, or any furniture a baby can reach.

At one time or another, either we or Jenny tried most of those remedies. The result: none produced any consistent relief from the pain.

Those gels that are supposed to soothe a baby's gums are the universal first choice. They work—for about five seconds.

"The gel is a topical anesthetic," our doctor said. "It numbs the outer surface of the gum. Unfortunately, the pain is coming from inside the gum."

The gels also have the usual handy-dandy array of chemicals, including propylene glycol, one of the ingredients in the coolant you use for your car's engine (you can look it up). And, in spite of all their flavorings, they taste horrible—try some.

We tried the folklorists' favorite, whiskey on the gums, just once; it didn't work. I suspect if we had done it often enough, Jenny would have absorbed enough alcohol to fall asleep; that's probably the real reason whiskey became a widely used teething remedy. We weren't about to do that, though we were assured that if we just "dotted" her gums, with a quick tap of the finger, there wouldn't be enough alcohol for Jenny to absorb into her system. Maybe we were being nutty parents again, but it still didn't feel right to us.

All the other remedies either were ineffective, or didn't appeal to Jenny's tastes, or were too hard on her sore gums. What next?

One remedy with some effect was infants' Tylenol; more than once, Jenny stopped crying as soon as she saw the dropper coming her way. But usually, it took a while for the relief to settle in. The painful crying brought back memories of the early days, when we held and carried Jenny through hours and hours of crying, day and night. How did we get through those times? Now we knew why she was crying, and we wanted to cry with her.

The only consistently effective remedy for teething pain was nursing. Joan tried to nurse Jenny as often as needed during teething; the sucking action would usually soothe her. Unfortunately, teething pain does not restrict itself to daytime. Jenny woke up several times each night, leaving Joan worn out.

Since nursing was not in my own bag of tricks, I was left scrambling during the day. I kept a variety of the recommended remedies on hand, hoping to buy a minute or two. Between pain episodes, I was busy mopping up the constant drooling that accompanies teething. One of the great tests of fatherhood is to hold a baby aloft, watch a drip descend, and remain undaunted as it plops onto your face.

And then, just after Jenny was six months old—two incisors on the bottom, poking through and sprouting up!

Joan named them James and John, from an A. A. Milne poem (unrelated to teeth) that Jenny enjoyed hearing us read to her. Peace—until the two top incisors began coming in, about a month later. The top ones seemed slightly less traumatic than the bottom, but only slightly less.

Teeth top and bottom meant more pain, but this time it was Joan feeling the pain when Jenny tried out her new teeth while nursing. And Jenny put the bite on me one night, through my shirt and into my shoulder. Somehow, I avoided dropping her.

When she wasn't biting, Jenny became a tooth inspector. Any friend or relative was a candidate for inspection. Jenny would insert her fingers, pry open her patient's mouth and examine the entire array of teeth. All she needed was a mirror, a drill, and someone to do her billing.

Then a third bottom tooth began to sneak in, too, in the painful process we were told would last until Jenny was two or two-and-a-half years old. She would be getting her molars at that age, and we were told the molars were sometimes the most painful of all.

Just think: five baby teeth down, and only fifteen to go.

Touching

JOAN TOOK A DEEP, RELAXING BREATH AND SIGHED IT OUT. She sprinkled safflower oil onto her hands, and smiled down at Jenny.

Jenny's massage was about to begin.

Jenny virtually purred while Joan's hands moved soothingly over her legs and arms, tummy and back. Some massages would last longer than others, because a nine-month-old baby wants to get moving. But we loved having this kind of contact with Jenny. And Jenny thrived on it.

Touching was one of our most important means of communication with Jenny. Through touching, we tried to tell her that she was loved and wanted, that she was safe and secure, that she could depend on us for comfort, for food, for protection. From her early months of confusion and crying, into her next state of happy exploration, the one constant was touching. We were always in contact with Jenny.

With our "hands-on" personalities, Joan and I probably could not have been any other kind of parents. We certainly were encouraged to keep holding Jenny by the writings of Dr. William Sears, a beacon for us in Jenny's troubled first months.

But our feelings about caring for a baby had crystallized early in Joan's pregnancy, when we both read Dr. Ashley Montagu's *Touching: The Human Significance of the Skin*.

The skin is the largest organ system in the body, and the sense of touch is the earliest to develop in the human embryo. "Among the most important of the newborn infant's needs," writes Montagu, "are the signals it receives through the skin, its first medium of communication with the outside world." Touching and stroking stimulate all of a baby's vital functions, from digesting to breathing. In fact, a massage like the one we gave Jenny is used as therapy for premature babies.

Yet we are still cautioned by our culture about too much touching, holding, and carrying—especially of a crying baby. Why? Montagu traces this prejudice to a source he calls the "Dr. Spock" of the early twentieth century: *The Care and Feeding of Children* by Luther Emmett Holt, Sr., first published in 1894 and in even more widespread use by its fifteenth edition in 1935. Says Montagu: "It was in this work that the author recommended the abolition of the cradle, not picking the baby up when it cried, feeding it by the clock, and not spoiling it with too much handling."

Montagu contrasts this theory with the practical discoveries of the early twentieth century in European foundling hospitals, where generous amounts of holding, carrying, cuddling, and caressing dramatically increased the babies' survival rate. Previous mortality rates in the foundlings' first year had been consistently above 50 percent and sometimes close to 100 percent, the result of a mysterious and unexplained wasting away.

Why can touching make such a profound difference? Perhaps because we are born too soon.

The human baby is not born after nine months because it is ready: it is born because its head would soon be too large to pass through the birth canal. Most mammals are able to crawl or walk to their mother for food or protection at birth; a human baby does not have that capability for nearly nine months. So a human baby continues its gestation outside the womb for another nine months. It needs a protective, supportive environment, which Montagu calls, with a touch of humor, "a womb with a view."

And how did we create this environment for Jenny? By holding, carrying, cuddling, caressing, hugging. By touching.

Jenny was always attached to us. We never left her alone to cry through any pain. Joan and I weathered our own exhaustion and more than a little scoffing to give Jenny the attention she needed and deserved. We disregarded advice on letting Jenny become independent to develop her own "self-soothing" strategies. How many adults are adept at "self-soothing"? We believed that Jenny had to learn she could depend on us before she could learn to be independent.

Those who thought we would spoil Jenny could not be more wrong, though we probably spoiled ourselves. Touching works both ways, and we began feeling the loss as Jenny spent less time in our arms. I don't know how any father could feel closer to his child than I feel to Jenny, thanks to all our holding and hugging. I think we'll always have a special bond.

With all our touching, hugging, and holding, we brought Jenny to a special birthday: on the Labor Day weekend of 1990, Jenny did her first genuine crawling, full speed ahead, making a declaration of independence just before she was nine months old.

Our toothy, crawling, laughing little explorer was ready to enter the world, on her own terms, on her own hands and knees. We gave her a special happy birthday hug, with many more to come.

Getting Control

The Feeding Follies

MY MOM SWORE SHE FED ME BEETS ONLY ONCE, and she said I was too young to remember.

Either I was older than she recalled, or she fed them to me a second time, because I did remember beets.

I could picture beets being wedged between my teeth. I could visualize the hateful beets splattered purple and dripping on the wall, and I knew exactly how they had gotten there. I had spit them there, and I was glad to have done it.

As we ventured into the unknown realm of solid food with Jenny, I checked our walls regularly: they remained unstained, though beets weren't on the menu. If it were my decision, they would never be on the menu.

But since Joan was directing Jenny's diet and preparing much of her food, I knew beets were an eventuality we would just have to swallow. Joan loves beets. And according to the schedule we were using, Jenny would soon be ready for beets, as soon as she reached the age of ten months. I dreaded the day.

In the pre-beets days, feeding Jenny was hardly traumatic, but it was far from simple. Remember that Jenny was always a picky eater, right from her first days of exasperating Joan with short, frequent nips of breast milk. Joan said Jenny ate like a hummingbird. We adjusted from feeding her three meals a day to three smaller meals and a number of snacks; she never seemed to take much at a sitting. And when she lost interest in taking food in, she took a great interest in putting it on—her hands, face, neck, head, hair. More than once, I found some in her ear.

For more efficient mealtimes, I devised the "Multiple Spoon System."

The challenge: while being fed, Jenny liked to take hold of the spoon for herself, either to help with feeding or to inspect the food. She especially enjoyed research in green foods, like peas and green beans. If they were paired with something orange, like butternut squash, Jenny would turn eating time into face-painting time.

The solution: using two spoons, and sometimes three. When

Jenny grabbed one spoon, I had another ready so I could continue feeding her without missing a pass. If she became a two-fisted spoon-grabber, I could still outmaneuver her with a third spoon (if I had remembered to have a third spoon ready).

The Multiple Spoon System was an unqualified success, meaning it actually worked about three times. The rest of the times we just kept at it, trying and hoping, adding little wrinkles like repeating one of her favorite words (a comically stretched-out "zucchini") to prompt a smile and an open mouth.

Another (occasionally) foolproof method was to serve Jenny her favorite foods: pears, summer squash, or butternut squash. She was so fond of pureed pears that I couldn't get the spoon from the dish to her mouth quickly enough. She'd strain her head forward, open her mouth wide, and practically inhale the pears.

I couldn't blame her: the pears were delicious. That was our most pleasant discovery in preparing most of Jenny's meals ourselves: using fresh fruits and vegetables, homemade baby food actually did taste good. We even used some of the recipes for our own meals; we loved the pureed butternut squash. With the simplest of preparations, everyday fruits and vegetables like pears or plums, squash or peas, could become treats verging on delicacies.

We waited until Jenny was six months old to feed her solid foods, to make sure her digestive system had matured (and yes, some eyebrows were raised over the way we did that, too). Rice cereal was the unanimous recommendation for her first food, followed by other simple grains. But what foods should come next, and in what order?

Help came from a book called *Mommy Made (and Daddy, Too!): Home Cooking for a Healthy Baby and Toddler*, by Martha and David Kimmel with Suzanne Goldenson. The Kimmels' well-researched cookbook and nutritional guide had its genesis in a discovery identical to one Joan and I made: most baby food in jars tastes miserable. If someone spooned that stuff into our mouths, we'd spit it out, too. The Kimmels started making food for their own baby, then went commercial with "homemade" baby foods.

The recipes were simple, usually steaming followed by pureeing in a food mill or food processor. Jenny reached the age of six months in mid-June; summer, of course, is prime time for fresh fruits and vegetables. We would load up with goodies during Saturday morning trips to a farmers' market set up in a school parking lot on Chicago's North Side. Then we'd go home and prepare the foods (Joan did the cooking, I did the pureeing) and freeze them in individual portions. Out of a wide range of fresh foods, Jenny turned down only sweet potatoes and peaches, and even those rejections were mild.

Imagine how healthy we would be if we could stick to Jenny's original diet: cereal, fresh fruit, and fresh vegetables. As a growing baby, she did need fat in her diet—but she got exactly the right kind of fat from breast milk. All fresh foods, no junk foods, no cholesterol problems. And the taste? Wonderful—except for beets, of course.

Beets. There was no avoiding them. I couldn't keep them off the menu, even though I saw a bad omen forming: Jenny had begun blowing bubbles through some of her food. Still, Jenny had to make up her own mind.

Which she did, at exactly ten months, when Joan spooned the first beets into her mouth. Jenny smiled and wanted more.

So I tasted defeat on the beets. But I still had my principles, and I held out for a compromise: Jenny could have beets any time she wanted them—as long as somebody else fed them to her.

Time for Fun

THE GUESTS AROUND THE DINNER TABLE grew suddenly silent, leaving one voice hanging in the air: a high-pitched voice pretending to come from a stuffed animal; a silly falsetto striving for a little girl's attention.

My voice.

"Well, you do silly things when you're a father," I said. No one argued with me.

My only defense was the truth. If I did silly things, Jenny might laugh at them. And if Jenny was laughing, I didn't care how silly I looked.

Jenny had one of the grandest laughs I'd ever heard. If I were a stand-up comic, I'd pay to plant her in the audience. She'd throw her head back and laugh with her whole body and soul, her whole belly.

Was this the same little girl who cried continually her first six months? Now she would put as much of herself into her laughter as she once put into her crying. Jenny crinkled up her face with so much mirth, I started checking for laugh lines in the corners of her eyes and across the bridge of her nose.

Here's how easy it was: Make a funny face—laughter. Make a funny noise, a sudden movement—more laughter. Bore into her with kisses on her tummy, sides or back—the most laughter. But beware of telling the same joke twice (or making the same face or noise), because you'd get an "I've-already-heard-that-one" look. She only wanted fresh material.

But with reading, repetition was a plus. Jenny enjoyed her favorite stories with the same exuberance every day. Did I ham it up? What do you think?

Let's get to our favorite part of "Us Two," a poem by A. A. Milne: "'SHOO, Silly old dragons!' And off they FLEW!" With a great whooping and waving of arms, I could always get a giggle out of Jenny. No one ever appreciated my acting talent the way Jenny did. She liked my singing and dancing, too.

So what did I care if I got curious looks from the neighborhood burghers, as I sang the complete works of Raffi while wheeling Jenny along in her stroller? What did they expect, *The Barber of Seville?* All that mattered to me was Jenny's toothy smile when I launched into an operatic "Baby Beluga."

And our days weren't complete without working on our moves to some vintage rock and roll. Even the thought of dancing made me feel silly, until I discovered how much Jenny enjoyed it. We were spinning the radio dial one day when some twenty-year-old music took me back to light-hearted days of youth. Without thinking, I began spinning Jenny around the floor—and she loved it. Thanks to my discovery with Jenny, I gave Joan quite a turn at a wedding reception when I broke out my new flash on the dance floor. Take a powder, Patrick Swayze.

Jenny and I still did most of our rug-cutting on our hands on knees, but we did graduate to crawling races. If she was aiming at a spot where she wasn't supposed to go, she'd turn her head back toward me with an impish little smile, and then take off. I'd race her on hands and knees and head her off before she could bang her head or grab something fragile or threatening. I always won.

We did plenty of wrestling, too, especially at dressing and changing times. No more lying back calmly while Dad switched her diapers or put on a coverall: now I had to pin her. I'd get Jenny in a half-Nelson with a T-shirt, but she'd break free and put me in a nose hold. I'd grab a toe hold while chasing her with a diaper, but she'd retaliate with a scissors kick. Usually we ended up in a draw, with a rematch scheduled immediately.

There wasn't much humor while we struggled through Jenny's painful and exhausting early months. Joan and I didn't eat dinner together for nearly six months; we ate in shifts, with one of us holding Jenny. I know our glum outlook was all too clear to see. We were longing for the fun times to arrive.

But when the fun began, I still had to lose that tightly buttoned part of me that never wanted to look silly, even when I was a kid. If I couldn't risk being silly with my own baby girl, when would I ever find a better excuse?

To my surprise and delight, the payback was immense. One especially long day, when Joan had to stay late at work, I took Jenny out for another stroll in the early evening. I was moping along with my head down, before glancing at Jenny in the stroller. She had been waiting to catch my eye. She gave me the happiest six-toothed smile I could ever have imagined.

I hugged her, and got her laughing with a kissing attack. I didn't know whether anyone could see us, and I didn't care.

Jenny's Home

BEFORE JENNY WAS BORN, she had something waiting for her that I never had when I was growing up: a room with a door and a window, a room that could become her own little world.

She was a lucky little girl, and I was happy for her.

I did have a room when I was a kid, but it was always a passageway to another room. Our five- and six-room apartments in Brooklyn were laid out in a straight line ("railroad flats," they were called). You walked through every room to get from the front of the apartment to the back.

The only place you could close the door on the rest of the apartment was the bathroom. If you wanted solitude, you went into the bathroom. Or you went out.

As a kid, I became fascinated by people who lived in "real" houses—meaning the people in the TV family shows of the 1950s and 1960s.

Our only comparable view of a working-class family in New York City was "The Honeymooners." The Kramdens' address was near ours on Chauncey Street, and watching them in close quarters was like peering through a neighbor's window. But even Ralph and Alice had a door on their bedroom.

Other TV families—the Cleavers, the Stones, the Andersons, the Nelsons, even the ex-Brooklynite Rileys—lived in mythic, affluent lands like California, producing weekly culture shock. Their houses—all ideal single-family dwellings—didn't lean out over the curbs: they were fifty feet back from untrafficked, tree-lined streets. They all had two-acre front lawns, and back yards, and driveways, and garages with basketball hoops. Inside, all the TV houses had more doors than I had ever seen in my life. And stairs: what was it like to live in a place with stairs? Not to mention more than one bathroom!

All the kids had their own rooms, with windows, and with neat stuff on the walls, and doors—on the second floor, yet. With a stern father's look, Ward Cleaver would say: "Theodore, I'm afraid you'll have to go to your room." Beaver would react with a face as long as the Cleavers' driveway. I used to think: "Hey, Beaver! Take a walk, and I'll go to your room instead." I would have felt rewarded, unless the room needed cleaning.

Joan had that kind of welcoming room, in that kind of spacious house, when she was a girl. If I had seen her big house, her big family, and her little New Jersey town when I was a kid, they would have seemed as real to me as a TV show. In some ways, they still do.

Without an emotional tie like Joan's to a house-as-home, I looked outward. I thought of the city as my home. By the fifth grade, I was riding public transportation to school every day, and I was an able traveler before I was a teenager. Then, libraries, schoolyards, ballgames, movies, museums—all became favorite rooms in my extended home.

Looking back, I realize how diligent my parents were in creating a family life for us in sometimes-difficult circumstances. But our life did not center on home as a place we loved. The places we lived were places I always anticipated leaving. I don't know if any of them is still standing, and I've never cared enough to go back and see.

Joan's feelings couldn't have been more different. She remembers her house as a treasured member of her family. Her house had a history, a personality, a character beyond shelter.

I didn't understand the strength of Joan's connection to her house until we visited New Jersey shortly after we were married. My folks had recently moved there, into the first house they ever owned. We took a detour to Joan's home town, and drove to her old family home.

The new owners had carved it up into office spaces.

Joan was overcome with emotion. She mourned her loss. She loved that big, old house, and she would always think of it as her home.

I wouldn't trade the way I grew up: I liked being a city kid, and I'd like Jenny to have a city kid's savvy. But I'd also like Jenny to feel that her home is a cherished place, as Joan did. She already has a room with a door and window, with pictures on her walls, even her own rainbow. It's on the second floor, too. Nobody has to walk through her room to get somewhere else. She's lucky.

I feel lucky living here, myself. But for Jenny to love our house as a home, she must love the life she has here. If we can give her that kind of life, she will always love her home. All of us will.

We're Number Two

EACH MONDAY, I began the week by becoming chopped liver.

Joan would try to leave for work Monday morning after Jenny had had her around in limitless supply all weekend. Naturally, Jenny saw nothing special about Monday and wanted Mom to stick around. So she whimpered in my arms, straining to get to Joan, while Joan was trying to edge out the back door.

Joan would take her and hold her, then give her back to me. Then Jenny would be really upset.

Joan and I would try to comfort her. Joan would give Jenny a smile and ask: "Hey, what's your Dad, chopped liver?"

Since Jenny might cry most of a Monday morning after Joan left, the obvious answer seemed to be: "Yes, Dad is chopped liver." It become a running family joke, and I'd go along with a tight smile.

At this stage, around ten months, Jenny had a heightened awareness of who Joan and I were, when we were around, and when we were gone—even if we had just left the room to wash our hands. And she knew beyond doubt that she had a unique relationship with her mom. Even though Dad was the one who was around most of the time, Mom was definitely Number One and Dad was Number Two. Whether permanent or temporary, that judgment made it difficult for all of us, especially for me.

Let's go to Monday afternoon. After a difficult morning, Jenny had settled back into her usual happy self. She and I were laughing again. Joan had been home for her lunchtime visit and gone back to work, and Jenny maintained her equilibrium. Meg, our babysitter, had arrived after school at 3:00 P.M., and Jenny spent a delighted two hours with her. They were pals, and mom-separation anxiety didn't seem to apply to pals.

At 5:00 P.M., I'd take Jenny back and she would be delighted to see me. We'd wave goodbye to Meg, babble to each other for a couple of minutes, and go back indoors. And then: Jenny would focus on the back door, waiting for Joan to appear. She'd be squirmily unhappy until Joan got home. Her anxiety about her mom's return was never far from the surface.

When Joan came home, Jenny tried to spring from my arms into hers. If Joan tried to go upstairs for a change of clothing or a rest stop, Jenny got upset. If I didn't keep Jenny within sight or sound of Joan, she cried.

Just a stage, I kept telling myself. Don't take it personally.

But I was the one who had changed some 2,500 diapers in those ten months. I was the one who'd been right there with Jenny every day. I was the one who'd gotten her through all these mean blue Mondays.

And I was the one who broke my own record for "marathon carrying" on a Monday morning. I held Jenny through tears and a nap for two hours and twenty minutes, walking back and forth from the front of the house to the back, marking time on the kitchen clock. I tried to put her down twice, and twice she would have nothing to do with being put down, so I trudged on.

Jenny got the long nap she needed. I got a three-day backache. Yet, I was chopped liver—even on weekends. When Jenny had her mom around, she didn't want to miss a minute with her—or waste a minute with me.

This dad business could be tough. I had to remind myself of a very different time.

In Jenny's early months of ceaseless nursing and relentless crying, she often would calm down only in my arms. She would go to sleep at night only if I carried her or rocked her, beginning with the first night after her birth.

Exhausted from sleepless nights and constant nursing, Joan felt denied of even the simplest rewards. More than once, Jenny's apparent choice left Joan in tears. "If I wasn't feeding her," Joan said, "she wouldn't need me at all." Of course, this wasn't true, but knowing it wasn't always enough to ease Joan's hurt.

In both cases, Jenny was simply trying to fulfill different needs the best way she could during a confusing time. At this point, she was trying to sort out the meaning of her mom's comings and goings. She was acutely aware of how well she knew—or didn't know—everyone she saw, and she was not hesitant about expressing her distrust when a person or situation loomed as a threat. Mom was the one she trusted most, needed most, and wanted most. Dad was nice, but he wasn't Mom.

He's not chopped liver, either, even if he sometimes felt that way. I could understand that Jenny needed to sort out her anxieties over the separation from Joan. But this stage gave me some serious anxieties of my own.

Different Worlds

WHEN I THOUGHT OF JENNY AS A CHILD of the twenty-first century, I wondered if she would think of her parents as antiques.

Consider the questions she may someday ask: "Daddy, what was the Berlin Wall? Did you really do math homework without a computer? What did people do at night before Nintendo? How did savings banks work? Why don't you speak Japanese?"

The world Joan and I entered forty-plus years ago will be difficult for her to comprehend. When we were among the early arrivals in the postwar "Baby Boom," Harry Truman was in the White House, Joe Stalin was in the Kremlin, and Mao Tse-tung was poised to begin the Great Leap Forward in Beijing (back then, it was Peking).

"Joltin' Joe" DiMaggio had not yet "left and gone away," as Simon and Garfunkel would one day lament; the Yankee Clipper still roamed center field at Yankee Stadium. Black America turned its lonely eyes to Brooklyn, where Jackie Robinson, Branch Rickey, and the Dodgers were changing baseball and the nation forever.

TV shows were live, if you were one of the fortunate few with a TV set; most evenings were still spent huddled around the radio. Movie theaters had one big screen, not six small ones, and double features changed every week. Watching movies at home meant Uncle Joe was showing blurry 8 mm films of his Florida vacation, projected onto a bed sheet hung on the wall. Car phones were science fiction. People still had party lines.

Japan and Germany were occupied nations, and the Allies were airlifting food and supplies into West Berlin to thwart a Soviet blockade. The question igniting Washington, D.C., was "Who lost China?" Joe McCarthy was a new U.S. senator from Wisconsin; John F. Kennedy, a new congressman from Massachusetts; Richard Nixon, a new congressman from California. Veteran Texas congressman Lyndon Johnson was new to the U.S. Senate. Adlai Stevenson was governor of Illinois, Dwight Eisenhower was president of Columbia University, and the city of Chicago had not yet elected a Daley as mayor. French Indo-China had not yet become Vietnam.

The United States and the USSR were the world's only atomic powers. The United States was on its way to developing the "ultimate weapon," the hydrogen bomb. ENIAC, the first electronic digital computer, had recently been built at the University of Pennsylvania. A new Chevrolet cost less than $1,000.

As a twenty-first-century child, Jenny may find it incredible that Joan and I had tangible links to the nineteenth century and the "old country." She may learn that immigrants thought America's streets were paved with gold; her great-grandparents believed strongly enough in that America to leave their homes and pursue that dream.

Joan's grandmothers both were born in 1878 (when Ulysses S. Grant was president). Her paternal grandmother was born in County Mayo, Ireland; her maternal grandmother, born in New York City, lived almost until her hundredth birthday. My paternal grandfather was born in Sicily in 1891. He landed at Ellis Island in 1910, and saw Buffalo Bill in a Wild West show at Coney Island. He was alive when Wilbur and Orville Wright made their first flight in 1903, and he lived to see astronauts walk on the moon. He saw two world wars. He spoke no English when he came to America, and he dug ditches when he could find work, but two of his grandchildren went to college.

The changes during our own lives have been no less dramatic. Joan and I were among millions of children rescued from the threat of polio by the Salk vaccine. We scrambled under our desks at school during "take cover" drills in the 1950s, hiding from nuclear attack, and we lived through the Cuban missile crisis. We saw the Berlin Wall put up—and we also saw it torn down. We saw the leader of the Soviet Union win the Nobel Prize for peace, then we saw the dissolution of the Soviet Union, the thawing of the Cold War, and the tragic dismemberment of Eastern Europe.

Jenny will be growing up in a nastier world than the one Joan and I roamed as children, with the insidious influence of drugs and violence now at every level of society. We only had "the bomb" worrying us, not semiautomatic weapons fire at the corner.

Can we solve the crisis in our educational system before Jenny goes to school? Will we come to terms with our national debt before she is working and paying taxes? Can we stop AIDS as we stopped polio? Can we end the shame of homelessness in the midst of our country's wealth?

A troubling future, perhaps. But think of the startling changes during our grandparents' lives; think of the changes during the last forty years; think of the changes just in 1990 alone, during Jenny's first year. As many troubling questions as the future holds for Jenny, it also holds this possibility: she may help to answer some of those questions.

Let's Talk, Already!

After all my coaching in "Da-da" and "Dad-dee" for ten months, Jenny edged relentlessly toward saying "Mommy" first.

Standing in her crib after Joan had left for work, Jenny made what sounded like a request: "Uh-mmmeeeee. Mmmmmm-meeeee." And in my arms, after Joan came home at the end of the day and dashed upstairs for a quick change of clothes, Jenny seemed to be pleading: "Uh-mmmeeee! Mmmmmm-meeeee!"

If that wasn't "Mommy," what else would it be?

In a sense, it didn't have to be anything. We always are in danger of projecting our own interpretations onto a child's prelingual sounds.

Some of Jenny's favorite pretalk expressions were (approximately): "Bah. Uh-bah. Uh-buh. Buh. Buh-buh. Bwah. Bwah?" Hearing those phrases one day, someone who didn't know Jenny well gave this immediate translation: "Oh! She wants her bottle!"

Now, of course, you'll remember that Jenny never, never took a bottle, from those earliest days of trying to punch it out of my hand. So it was highly unlikely she ever would ask for a bottle, let alone make "bottle" her first attempt at a word—unless she was trying to say: "Get that stupid bottle out of here!"

Yet for all her musical sounds and lilting phrases that floated just beyond our understanding, Jenny had a surprisingly sharp sense of what we were saying to her.

In the morning, while crawling around on our bed, Jenny would understand our question: "Where is the FAN, Jenny?" She'd look up until she located the ceiling fan, one of her favorite sights since her earliest days. She'd smile. And when we'd say, "See the fan go a-ROUND, and a-ROUND, and a-ROUND," she'd smile even more widely.

When Joan would ask: "Where's DADDY?" Jenny would turn and look at me, so she knew "daddy" even if she couldn't (or wouldn't) say the word. Naturally, we regarded her as brilliant.

As much as we might like one, there is no program for a child's talking. Clear words, and even phrases, may emerge well before the age of one year. Or there may be no words at all until the advanced age of three years (a friend of ours says that's how long it took him to start talking, and he has compensated for the delay by talking nonstop since then).

But these exciting little glimpses of communication could feed our impatience—especially mine. I wanted more—now! I was eager to talk to Jenny and have her talk back to me, in ways I could understand. I wanted to know what Jenny was thinking, what she was feeling, how she saw the world.

Joan tells me I am a patient man, but my impatience always has been a big troublemaker for me. I can't count the bad choices I've made because I wasn't willing to wait a bit longer, to get bit more information, or to sort out my emotions a bit more clearly. Then I would (mentally) kick myself and think: "I need more patience—right away!" Will the lesson ever sink in?

Impatience can intensify your dilemma as a new parent. You have to raise a baby with a philosophy of long-term reward, because immediate rewards are not always easy to find—or appreciate—in the early days. Yet you need some short-term rewards to be able to go the distance.

Maybe that's why babies are so surprising: it's their most effective way to reach us and get us on their side. Unexpected rewards often are the finest.

While all my "Da-da" prompting appeared to be getting no results, Jenny startled us one night with an unexpected development when she was about nine-and-a-half months old. Joan was reading a book to her, and Jenny began turning the pages.

No ripping, no tearing, just an orderly flipping of pages. Here was the result of reading several stories to Jenny each day. While I was focused on whether or not Jenny was learning to talk, she actually had learned how to "read," by watching us move from page to page and understanding the progression of the book.

Now when I read to Jenny, she would turn every page. I'd help her, of course, so that she'd turn only one page at a time and not six or a dozen. Each page was a reward, a greater reward for being so unexpected, and for being such a clear indication that Jenny was setting her own direction and determining the pace of her own development.

Her own pace always will be the right pace, despite our impatience. When will she talk? When will she walk? When will she sleep through the night? All the answers to these questions are the same: when she is ready.

When Jenny was ready, she would choose her own first word. I knew I would be delighted, whatever the choice. But I was still hoping for "Daddy."

A Woman's World

IF SOMEONE HAD TOLD ME when I was single that there was a way I could spend most of my time around women, I would have said: "Where do I sign?"

As Jenny's at-home father, I signed a long-term contract.

When I was a sportswriter, I was at home in a world as totally male-dominated as our culture will tolerate today. Now I was spending all day with my ten-month-old daughter. And there were few opportunities for sports dialogues with Joan: when she went to the 1983 All-Star Game at Comiskey Park, she brought a book to read.

I will spend my future growing accustomed to having a child who wears dresses of all kinds on all sorts of occasions. Mostly, at this stage, I dressed her in comfortable pullover shirts and overalls—but all in bright or flowery colors. I was already practiced at putting tights on her, and putting bows in her hair.

I had to admit that the fancy "girl" stuff could be fun to put on her, because Jenny looked so pretty in it. And she already liked to pull clothes out of her dresser drawers, so she may share Joan's passion for clothes.

That's just life at home. In the wide world beyond, however, I was discovering that there were women everywhere. I never knew there were so many women.

They seemed to feel less awkward with me than I did with them. They appeared to enjoy seeing a man taking care of a baby. Maybe they thought: "Hey, there's a man who understands what it's like!" Some women even compared notes with me, almost like one mom to another. Believe me, it's a uniquely intimate experience for a man to discuss breastfeeding with a woman he has just met.

We'd usually meet on the playgrounds, at the swings, with conversation beginning this way: "How old is your little girl? How much does she weigh? How is she sleeping? How are you sleeping? How many teeth does she have? Is she walking? Talking?"

If our babies were breastfed, we'd spot each other—and the babies—right away. The breastfed babies were slimmer, with more color in their cheeks. After asking, "Is your baby breastfed?" (just to be sure), we'd discuss the weight issue. Bottle babies seemed twice as big and round; breastfed babies tended to fall off the low end of the weight curve on the pediatricians' growth charts. So we'd reassure each other about how great our breastfed babies looked, and how inappropriate those growth charts were.

Reassurance is important. One mom, with a daughter about Jenny's age, said apologetically: "She might take more naps, but I could never bring myself to put her down and leave her to cry herself to sleep. I just couldn't listen to her cry like that."

"I think that's the best feeling a parent can have," I said, "not being able to shut out your child's crying. I think it's the best thing you can do, to be there for your child when she's crying."

She felt better, and I felt great.

Yet there was no escaping a little hierarchical comparison, and not just of weight or development. "Oh, is she walking?" I was asked one day on the playground, "I see her socks are dirty." I began describing Jenny scampering around in her little rolling walker, then realized the salient point was not a developmental stage, but simply dirty socks.

There seemed to be no escape from this woman's world. At one summer party, instead of talking baseball with the guys, I wound up talking babies with a grandmother. Fascinated, I heard her describe creating toys from wooden spoons and oatmeal containers. And diapers? She made them herself.

On another planned escape, I went to a Chicago White Sox game at old Comiskey Park with a group from Joan's office (Joan and Jenny were home). I fantasized a night spent drinking beer and talking baseball. I discovered I was seated between a woman (and mom) who taught art to children, and a woman expecting her second child in two weeks.

So instead of drinking beer and talking baseball, I again wound up talking babies. After a few innings to adjust, I was reveling in the support and attention these women gave me for my unconventional role as a father. The game was forgettable, but the experience was memorable.

In this new world of mine, women created surprises everywhere. I was carrying Jenny in a front pouch one day, walking around the neighborhood, when we passed an elderly woman rolling her laundry home in a cart. The woman looked at me and Jenny, and with a stern face said something quietly in Italian—to me or to herself, I wasn't sure which.

My Italian has nearly rusted away. I thought she was saying something like: "You are really crazy." A half-block later, I realized what she actually had said: "You are a good father."

Those words felt like a tribute, coming from a woman.

A Man and a Father

WHEN I TOLD BOB WHY I WAS LEAVING MY JOB, he gave me one of those looks and laughs usually reserved for a guy wearing one shoe, a layer of dirt, and two pairs of pants, screaming at passing cars. "What are you, crazy?" he said, then he shrugged. "Well, if that's what you want to do . . ."

I could see him mentally writing me off as he went to join the rest of the party noisily filling the ballroom at the Sheraton Centre in Montreal, the late-night farewell gathering after Calgary's sixth-game victory over the Montreal Canadiens to capture the 1989 Stanley Cup.

It was also a personal farewell for me, the night I told my friends in the hockey media the full story of my career switch to being an at-home father.

Bob was the only one of my old sportswriting pals who tossed his doubts at me. Maybe the rest were masking their honest reactions, but I doubt it. They were all surprised; they had to be, after knowing me all those years when I was in love with life on the road. But one after another, they gave me their enthusiastic best wishes. Some, veteran parents as well as veteran journalists, counseled me on how hard it might be. Others told me how great it would be, as Keith Gave of Detroit had said while we were walking back from the Forum along a quiet Ste. Catherine Street after we finished writing about the Cup-winning game.

"So you're going to be a 'Mr. Mom,'" said Keith, one of the first to label me as such. "That's fantastic. You're going to love it. I spent a lot of time with my son when he was born and I loved every minute of it. And it'll be great if you write about it."

The women I told about the change were unanimous: they were even more enthusiastic than the men. But some time later, I provoked a wistful reaction from my boss when I handed him my resignation letter over lunch. He told me about an incident during his family's summer vacation in Italy.

"We were having one of those arguments that a family can get into," he said, "and my wife told my son, 'Ask your dad.' And my son said, 'How would Dad know? He's never around.' I've always put in a lot of time at work—nights, long days, weekends. It's what the job demands. But I know over the years I've missed an awful lot with my kids."

I was always determined to avoid that empty spot in my life. I never wanted to look back with regret for time lost with Jenny. I know my father felt that way about time lost when my sister and I were young, when he was working two jobs and putting in long hours at night and on weekends.

I've been able to use time in a way that my father wasn't able to use it; I've been fortunate enough to have the time that he never had. And I know he appreciates the kind of father I am, and the kind of parents Joan and I strive to be. We got the message in a phone conversation after my parents had returned home from visiting us, during the hard early months filled with so much of Jenny's pain and crying.

"We were talking about you during the plane ride home," my mother said. My father continued, "You two just go and go to the point where other parents would stop, and then you just keep on going. I think you two are about the most caring parents I've ever seen."

No support is ever more valuable than the support of our families, the people we have loved the best and the longest. I've always felt that support as strongly from Joan's family as I have from my own; in fact, I don't even feel that I differentiate any more between "my family" and "Joan's family."

No one could have asked for or anticipated more understanding, support, and encouragement than we've gotten from our family and friends—both for Joan and me as parents, and for me in my nontraditional role. In fact, I've even had something of a family "role model." My brother-in-law, Paul, was home with his daughter, Kate, during her second three months—and he did it without pay. A free-lance graphic artist, he has since been able to spend a lot of time at home regularly with Kate, who is also blossoming as an artist at the age of seven.

I may have become a role model myself during all of my walks around the neighborhood with Jenny during her first two years; at least, Jenny has become a local celebrity. Almost everybody in the neighborhood knows her and greets her, especially the older people sitting on their stoops and leaning out their windows.

But of all the reactions I've encountered to being an at-home father, one still haunts me: the sad face of our neighbors' little son, looking down at me and Jenny from his second-floor window.

During the day, he was in the charge of a "nanny" who spoke virtually no English, who sat around and watched while he played in front of the house with a notable lack of spirit. Once, in the evening, his mother brought him into our yard, ostensibly to let him play with our wind chimes, which had been melodious in a spring breeze. In the times that followed, she seemed a little more honest about her son's motivation: "He calls you 'the other daddy.' He said he wanted to come over and see 'the other daddy.'"

His own daddy liked to drink and talk loud and scold his son. I always hoped that was as far as it went. Long after this family sold their house and moved away, I still hoped they were all doing better, especially that sad-faced little boy.

Whatever mistakes I've made, whatever mistakes I'll make, I know this: as long as I'm breathing, Jenny will never bring a sad face to the window, longing to visit "the other daddy." Of all the reactions people have to me as a father, Jenny's will always be the most important.

Getting Control

JOAN AND I were having one of our after-dinner, room-to-room conversations when a rock came flying at me in the kitchen.

Without malice, innocent of the effect, Joan had called me a "househusband."

"Don't ever call me that," I said. "I don't like it. Don't ever use that word again."

"Househusband" cut too close to the truth: I felt like a househusband, and I didn't like the feeling.

It was part of a larger feeling I had been experiencing each morning. I'd look at my face in the bathroom mirror and think: "Who is this guy? Whose pent-up, pinned-down life is this?" I felt as if I was living in one long episode of "The Twilight Zone," where I wasn't in control of anything, not even my own dialogue.

Joan could tell I was living in a different zone, and she was being left stranded. We had one of our late-night, face-to-face, heart-to-heart talks. My difficulties were increasing the pressure on her. If I was sunk, if I wasn't taking care of myself, we were all sunk. We needed some new solutions.

I went to work on the problem, but I was stymied. A morning "drop-in" center on the North Side wasn't practical because of traveling time. Another children's-and-parents' activities program was booked up for the current cycle.

So I devised my own solution: I ran.

On Wednesday mornings, Jenny had been staying with Joan's mom while I went to a health club. The exercise always improved my outlook. In fact, exercise is one of the body's most effective methods of combating the blues: get those long muscles working, and pump out those "feel-good" endorphins.

If exercise was good, more exercise would be better—and not just my "fathercize" program. It had to be solo, my own time for myself, every day.

Where would I fit it in? I'd never been an "early" person, but the only time left was the early morning. Since I was having a hard time recognizing my old self any longer, I figured one more change wouldn't be so difficult.

So I began to get out of bed every morning at 6:15, sneaking silently downstairs, struggling into sweat clothes, and slipping out the door. A couple of stretches and I'd start running. I'd never especially liked running. I didn't exactly look forward to it.

But my body would wake up. My head would clear. I'd think about the day ahead of me. I'd ponder The Meaning of Life. Back in the house, I'd skim the morning paper over breakfast cereal, then take a shower. I'd head back upstairs fully dressed by 7:30 A.M., ready to scoop up Jenny and let Joan begin her own day.

One immediate result was getting a shower every morning, which hadn't previously been dependable. By asserting some control over the day, claiming time for myself, I got a foot out of the Twilight Zone. I began to feel more like a person who was also a father, rather than a father who had once been a person. Surrounded by what seemed like domestic confusion, I had to develop a way to bring some part of my life under control. Physically more relaxed after my runs, I began to work on sorting out my emotional confusion. I needed some control there, too.

I was inventing the kind of parent I wanted to be. I had no model for it. I sometimes felt as if I was reacting before I realized what was happening and what I was feeling; it felt almost as if I was reacting from a separate part of myself.

Here's a guilt-ridden example: Jenny kicked her socks off one day while we were out for a walk. I found the socks quickly, but I also found myself quickly overreacting. "Jenny, keep your socks on!" I said angrily, and Jenny and I were equally shocked at my outburst.

I didn't want to react that way. Stress pushed a button, an old tape played, and out came the reaction. My models were old tapes that were recorded long ago in childhood, internal tapes of what I'd seen and heard throughout my life. The tapes always played back an old reaction faster than I could invent a new one.

Trying to change all the tapes at once would be overwhelming. If they played before I could stop them, my only remedy was to forgive myself. The first step in gaining control was realizing I couldn't always be in control. Then, if I worked on erasing those old tapes a bit at a time, I could begin replacing them with new ones, and begin feeling and behaving differently.

Slowly, deliberately, I began rerecording my old running tape that way: I would overcome my resistance not by training for a marathon, but by running for about fifteen minutes each morning.

Who was this guy, this early-morning runner? I still wasn't sure, but I decided to lose my worn old sneakers and go out and buy a pair of running shoes.

My first.

A Year and a Life

It Hurts

JENNY PULLED HERSELF UPRIGHT alongside the coffee table, holding on with one hand. She picked up a little book in her other hand, let go of the table to hold the book in both hands for a teetering second, and then—

Whoops.

The bruises were coming more quickly now. These were the beginning days of bumps, thumps, scrapes, and falls both big and little. Of tears, large and small. These were days we'd been warned about by all those voices of experience: "Oh, just wait until she starts..."

In this case: "... getting up and trying to walk."

And falling down.

Joan and I patrolled our home, moving little threats out of harm's way, but we knew we couldn't remove all danger from the life of our eleven-month-old Jenny. As she extended her mobility, she was bound to find new opportunities for collisions.

We had frightening visions of all her possible injuries—but we also learned our visions might not be frightening enough. Some friends were visiting one night, sitting around the living room, watching Jenny scamper and bounce. The mother of three daughters asked us: "Have you made any trips to the emergency room yet?"

Joan and I had immediate knots in our stomachs. Oh, no! Did we really have to look forward to emergency rooms?

Yes, we may have to. Hurts will happen, and already have happened. We would do anything to spare her from being hurt, yet in Jenny's early months, we were the main culprits: we always seemed to be perpetrating little hurts on her, hurts that felt like gaping wounds inside us.

Joan once nipped Jenny's fingertip while trying to cut her fingernails, and drew blood. Joan was inconsolable. I once put Jenny in her high chair, and closed the catch on the safety belt—and Jenny began screaming. I finally realized I had pinched her leg in the catch. She had an angry red pinch mark on her leg for days. I was ready to be led to the whipping post.

And those were just little hurts. I hated to think of Jenny needing a trip to an emergency room; I could still remember my own first visit. On a late-summer day when I was about five years old, I was running around with another kid playing "football" without a football. I bounced off him and into a wrought iron fence, hitting my face against the pickets. I didn't think I was hurt, but I noticed something red on my glasses. I touched it and it smeared. Then I got scared.

My mom and dad were at work, and I was staying with my grandmother. I ran inside, wailing: "Grandma, grandma, I got hurt!" She saw me and began wailing in French (she had emigrated from Alsace).

We had no car. There was no way for my mom or dad to get home. My uncle worked nights and lived nearby, and we hoped he was home, sleeping. My grandmother called him (by then her English had returned). He soon arrived, carried me out to his car, and drove off to the hospital. An improvised, blood-soaked bandage covered my left eye.

In the emergency room, I took stitches in my left eyebrow. I remember lying on the table with a cover over my head and a stinging feeling in my forehead. I still have the scar. But the scariest part of the day was knowing I would have to explain it all to my parents.

If Jenny must ever face such an ordeal, Joan and I decided, we wanted to be prepared. We resolved to make a dry run to the nearest hospital emergency room. But on the designated weekend, I got the flu and could barely stand up. An emergency-room trip was out, unless I was the patient. Joan brought Jenny in for a couple of visits while I was laid out. Jenny looked concerned, pointed to me, and said a quiet "Buh." She looked back at me as Joan carried her away.

I bounced back enough to take care of Jenny by Monday morning; when you're a parent, and your child needs you, your powers of recovery can be amazing.

Hoping for an easy time, I put Jenny down to let her crawl around on the living room rug. But instead of zipping toward the couch or table, Jenny turned around and crawled back toward me. She grabbed onto my pants legs, pulling herself upright. She looked up at me, her eyes asking: "Please hold me, Daddy?"

She had missed her dad, and she spent the morning propped happily against my left shoulder. Feeling her attachment, I felt ready to keep her there forever, and always be her protector.

If only it were that simple. I know I can't shield her from hurt; I might as well try to shield her from life. I can only hope all her hurts are small ones.

Seuss Abuse

FROM HER PERCH IN THE BACKPACK, Jenny watched over my shoulder as I began working on dinner.

"This is a squash, Jenny," I said. "First, we wash the squash. Then we cut the squash and dump the seeds. We dump the seeds because they don't fit our needs. We put the squash in a big glass dish, and a squash and a dish add up to a squish!

"But we don't squish the squash once we give it a wash. We cook it ten minutes in the microwave oven, so it's quite well done both below and aboven!"

We were experiencing another unfortunate case of Parental Seuss Abuse.

This syndrome is the result of repeated readings of children's books written by Dr. Seuss, a.k.a. Theodor S. Geisel, who composed nearly fifty of these sanity-snagging little tales before his death in 1991 at the age of eighty-seven.

Reading was always one of Jenny's favorite activities, and Dr. Seuss was her earliest favorite author. Reading was one of the few activities that settled her in one place for more than ninety seconds or so, propped in my lap, turning pages, and offering her own commentary. Reading also gave Joan or me a something of a break from constantly lurching around after Jenny and being on guard.

And it was always fun.

Dr. Seuss wasn't in my repertoire when I was a kid. *The Cat in the Hat* was published in 1957, beyond my learning-to-read years, but Dr. Seuss probably would have been too new and radical for our schools, anyway. Not to mention subversive: at the end of *The Cat in the Hat*, the brother and sister ponder whether to tell their returning mom about the cat's dance of destruction through their house. They conclude with an enticing ambiguity: "Well . . . What would YOU do if your mother asked YOU?"

Definitely too out-of-control for the public schools of my day.

Dr. Seuss always seemed new, though some of his stories were several decades old. Jenny's favorites were *Green Eggs and Ham* (1959), *Happy Birthday to You!* (1960), and the wonderfully wise

Oh, the Places You'll Go! (1990). I always loved reading them to her, over and over.

Except when I DIDN'T, as Seuss might have said. Because you can't go through endless repetitions of "Not in a house, not with a mouse. Not in a box, not with a fox," without having your eyes and brain feel like scrambled green eggs. Sometimes I realized I was reciting a story without looking at the words.

Why does my head spin over reading another? I don't know. Go ask your mother.

Yet another parental danger sign: the "Raffi Daffies."

Raffi is a bearded Canadian singer who wore Hawaiian shirts and bear-claw slippers while performing for children's audiences. He's divorced now, and he sings about environmental issues instead of children's themes; but his children's tapes kept us from self-destructing during many a car ride. Raffi offered a nice mix of classic kids' tunes (Joan's favorite was "Thumbelina," mine was "Morningtown Ride"), upbeat life lessons ("Everything Grows"), and delightful little anthropomorphic stories ("Baby Beluga").

But if I was brushing my teeth in the morning and the complete Raffi discography began running unbidden through my head, I knew I had the "Raffi Daffies." Especially when I got to little insanities like "Eight Piggies," with its Russian-hued, dirge-like melody by way of Mussorgsky. ("There were eight piggies in a row, Oh! Eight piggies in a row. Did they laugh? No, no! Did they cry? No, no! There were eight piggies in a row.") If Mel Brooks ever makes a children's movie, "Eight Piggies" could be on the sound track.

Variety is an effective weapon against this type of brain strain. Once Jenny began playing by herself for (comparatively) longer periods of time, we essentially converted her room into a giant playpen—lots of rug space for crawling and tumbling, enough shelves and furniture for nonthreatening climbing, and a rocking chair for a supervising Mom or Dad.

There, Jenny was free to romp, free of "No, no!" and free of being picked up and deposited in a less threatening spot. If she wanted me, she could crawl over at her own pace, pull herself up on my pants leg, and give the "pick me up" look. Or she could crawl over to the shelf, pull herself up, and begin browsing through her books, settling on one and flipping through the pages. I'd put her in my lap and read that book to her.

At this stage, when she clambered over to the bookshelf, she would usually select her favorite Dr. Seuss: *Oh, the Places You'll Go!*

And as always, I would let Jenny know what a good choice she'd made: "Congratulations! You've picked a great book that tells all about life and is worth a long look from thinkers of every which size, shape, and nation. It's the Dr. Seuss ultimate philosophy summation!"

Seuss Abuse, plain and simple.

Jenny's Tapes

THERE GO THE VEGETABLES, right into Jenny's hair.

Next: sweet potatoes, massaged into her eyebrows and forehead; cereal, packed onto her cheeks and dripping from her chin. Now Jenny waves her spoon in triumph, with a shriek and a smile, displaying rainbow teeth.

We have it all on tape. A few seconds to rewind, and we can see it again, right on our TV screen.

Scenes like this meal mean a child of today has greater potential for future embarrassment than any child ever born before. The reason is a two-pound invention called the camcorder. With it, we can capture all those moments we don't want to forget—and which Jenny may some day be forced to remember.

Here is Jenny crawling, eating, crying, babbling, screaming, and playing with her grandparents. Precious moments become instant archives. But these instant archives have a price: now a child must account for behavior almost from the moment of birth, because videotape lets no one off the hook.

Joan and I might be embarrassed by our own prehistoric baby pictures, but we are free of responsibility. So what if we were posed nude on a bearskin rug before some tacky background? We could always plead: "They made me do it. I was set up. I was framed."

What will be Jenny's defense as she views tapes of herself applying a food facial? She can't say she was set up for it. All we did was give her the food. She was captured being herself, poor kid. She'll have to plead that she was only a baby and didn't know what she was doing.

Tapes are not all. We have pictures, lots of them, taken with my trusty old single-lens-reflex camera. With Joan doing the filing, we've already filled one photo album, and more are waiting. All of Jenny's facial expressions, and most of her emotional states, are documented in full color. She turns hambone as soon as I reach for a camera.

The thirteenth of the month was our official picture day (Jenny was born on December 13). We compiled a month-by-month chronicle of her development: at six months, for example, she is sitting propped up on the couch with a pink blanket for backdrop, sitting up well enough to be left on her own.

I also captured her laughter and her exuberance in that photograph, one of the best I've ever taken. Seeing that picture, you want to scoop her up in your arms and hug her and laugh with her. That picture never will embarrass her.

On film or tape, we hope to relive irreplaceable moments. One photo has forever captured Jenny playing with Joan's mom; Jenny is reaching up to retrieve the sock her grandmother has placed on her head, as they smile at each other across three generations. On tape, Jenny is laughing and babbling with my dad during my parents' visit when she was six months old; Jenny giggles while her grandfather says with mock severity, "You better start listening to me!"

Yet some of the most heartwarming moments remain elusive. How could I record Jenny leaning over to give me a sudden kiss on the nose? Could a videotape depict my emotions reducing me to a puddle? I might have missed recording many of these moments, but Jenny never missed any of them.

Jenny was equipped with her own internal camera, constantly recording tapes that never will appear on a TV screen. They will produce little flashing images in her unconscious mind, vivid emotional pictures forming her most elemental view of her world: her feelings of being loved and wanted, of being valued and respected.

Over time, these emotional images will be edited into a major production: Jenny's self-image. Her subconscious VCR will play back tapes instructing her in self-esteem, and in her relations with us and with the people around her.

When we play back our videotapes, we'll be trying to reconnect with our emotions, reconstructing and reliving our memories. Our tapes recreate our past—but Jenny's internal tapes will create her future.

Her personality will have a million elements, and each element can develop in a million ways. But in moments of stress or crisis, of emotions good or bad, Jenny's tapes will play back to form her most basic reactions. Her identity as a person will be directed by what goes onto the tapes she is making now—tapes that can't be easily erased.

How important are those tapes? All I had to do to answer that question was to consider the importance of my own tapes, the difficulties I had with some of my own "distant replays" recorded long ago in my early life. Remember the incident of Jenny's lost sock and my lost temper? I remembered too clearly, and it drove home to me the long-term importance of Jenny's internal tapes.

So for Joan and me, there was no bowing-out of our long-running roles as parents. The show had to go on. Jenny's camera was always rolling.

"Ma-ma" Arrives

GOOD NEWS FOR JOAN: Jenny said "Ma-ma-ma-ma" before "Da-da-da-da."

Good news for me: the days of chopped liver were over.

Actually, neither Joan nor I had much stake in which of the two "name approximations" Jenny would babble first. Joan probably was hoping for "Da-da-da-da" more fervently than I was; she thought it would be a suitable reward for Jenny's at-home father.

And sure, it would have been satisfying to hear "Da-da-da-da" as Jenny propelled her rolling walker across the floor, or did her speed-crawls around the rug to find the day's new adventures. But I knew "Da-da" was coming eventually, and I'd already received ample consolation—though I'm a bit embarrassed to admit it resulted from Jenny being upset.

One drizzly evening after dinner, we were all in the kitchen, with Jenny roaming around in her walker. I bundled up the garbage and took the bag out the back door, through the garage, and out to the garbage pails.

Heading back to the house, I could see Jenny pressing against the glass of the storm door, looking out into the night. Once inside, I got a big greeting from her. I picked her up, and saw vestiges of tears.

"As soon as she saw you leave," Joan said, "she went whizzing over to the door. She stood there looking for you, and she was whimpering the whole time you were gone."

No more chopped liver. Joan and I again were full partners in Jenny's affections. Even with Joan close to her, Jenny still missed me—on as brief a disappearance as a trip outside with the garbage. I gave Jenny a big hug.

Now Jenny began coming to me for comfort on those blue Mondays, instead of making it painfully obvious that she wanted Mom after having her around all weekend. Jenny and I were building our best rapport ever, and it was during one of our fun times that "Ma-ma" appeared clearly.

Right around her eleventh-month "birthday," Jenny and I were laughing and babbling our way through some cereal. She was experimenting with different noises between spoonsful, adding in some lip-smacking, when out it came: "Ma-ma-ma-ma."

She turned it into a refrain while she was crawling, "walking," sitting, reading, eating, playing. She used it for a wide range of expressions, as with her many inflections and variations of "bah."

"Ma-ma" wasn't specifically aimed at Joan. Jenny wasn't specifically naming her; in that sense, she was not "speaking." But her babbling had entered a transition, where she would use sounds as names. A few specific inflections of "bah" clearly referred to "light." "Ma-ma-ma" and "muh-muh-muh" were a sort of continuous play-by-play of her exploratory crawling around the kitchen floor; they also seemed to be a commentary on her emotional state—happily busy, the way we sometimes hum or sing when enjoying our work.

It was hard to resist the lure of placing meaning on "Ma-ma." Joan's mom, with seven children and seven grandchildren, said she had never heard another child saying "Ma-ma" before "Da-da." Independently, she and I made similar interpretations: Jenny might have been saying "Ma-ma" first because "Da-da" was home with her all the time. "Ma-ma" was the source of change, the focus of interest: "Ma-ma" was going to work, "Ma-ma" was coming home, "Ma-ma" would be home today. Jenny heard the word more often, and "Ma-ma's" comings and goings were noteworthy events.

But...

Wasn't "Ma-ma" the more natural sound to come first? "Da-da" seemed like a more difficult sound to make, with the tongue placed against the gum behind the upper front teeth and the sound needing a carefully timed expulsion of breath. In *Babyhood*, child psychologist Penelope Leach admitted our knowledge of early speech is sketchy, but said, "We do know that the open-vowel cooing comes before the consonants are added, and that the consonants P, B and M are almost invariably the first ones added to them."

Then again, Leach said, "The first words almost always are the names of deeply loved people or animals or highly significant objects which give (babies) pleasure."

So Leach was inconclusive.

But we reached one certain conclusion: Jenny was happiest when all three of us were together, when she had both "Ma-ma" and "Da-da" close enough for playtime and hugs. She was careful to kiss each of us the same number of times when we were together. She'd give me two kisses, then turn to Joan and give her two.

She was speaking clearly then, and she was saying: "I love you both."

A Special Day

THIS DAY BEGAN DIFFERENTLY.

I read Jenny a special message from her pal, Dr. Seuss: "Today you are you! That is truer than true! There is no one alive who is you-er than you! Shout loud, 'I am lucky to be what I am! Thank goodness I'm not just a clam or a ham or a dusty old jar of sour gooseberry jam! I am what I am! That's a great thing to be! If I say so myself, HAPPY BIRTHDAY TO ME!' "

The book: Dr. Seuss' *Happy Birthday To You!* The day: Thursday, December 13, 1990. Jenny was a year old.

From the day Jenny was born, Joan knew how we would celebrate this first birthday. Gathering with Jenny on her special day were Joan and myself; Joan's younger sister, Kathy; and Joan's mom. We four had seen Jenny into the world, and we came together to share memories and relive that day. And we would not pass up a chance for singing, gift giving, and cake eating—and cake for Jenny, too.

Jenny may not have known why all this was going on, but she knew that she liked it.

We envisioned repeating this for as many years as we could. Birthday parties are fun, and we scheduled a big party over the weekend to share the celebration of Jenny's birth with as many friends and family members as we could fit into her grandmother's apartment. But we wanted to leave this December 13 to remember her birth, convening those of us who actually witnessed the event, keeping the day as special as we could.

Along with remembering Jenny's arrival on that cold, intense day, we wanted to celebrate Jenny as the person she had come to be. We always want to celebrate her for who she is, and not only because she is ours.

And just who is she?

Before Jenny was born, we imagined a perfect little blend of Joan and me. All her traits and characteristics would fall neatly into one category or the other: half from Joan, half from me. She would have Joan's eyes, and my ears; Joan's nose, and my mouth.

After Jenny was born, we sometimes played: "Whose kid is this?" Which of us did she favor when she began some special pursuit?

When Jenny steered her rolling walker toward the bookcase in the living room, the first book she pulled out was invariably *The Book of Garlic*. So she was definitely Joan's daughter; Joan believes deeply in the culinary value of garlic. But when Jenny headed over to the other bookcase, the book she pulled out and carried around was the *Simon and Schuster Pocket Guide to Beer*. Hey, that's my girl!

Jenny definitely had Joan's eyes: big, green, and expressive, with elements of gold and some days of gray or blue. She seemed to have my ears, but we had some concern over the future of her upturned little nose. "I hope she gets my nose," Joan told me. "Your nose looks fine on your face, but I don't think it would go well with her face." I agreed completely.

But where did Jenny get her golden hair? Joan and I are dark-haired, although Joan's hair was blonde until she was about two-and-a-half years old.

Jenny showed Joan's determination and exuberance in going after what she wanted. She showed my temper if she didn't get it.

Some traits were puzzling, or at least ambiguous. At one point, Jenny mastered the technique of grabbing hold of the frame of her rolling walker and lifting it so the two front wheels would clear the edge of the rug and not halt her progress.

Had she inherited my mechanical aptitude for analyzing the way things work? Or was she doing a "wheelie" to show that she had inherited Joan's driving style?

Playing "Whose kid is this?" was strictly for fun. Joan and I always knew that most of Jenny was pure Jenny, and for that we could not have been happier. She was her own little person, growing more complex each day. Five traits from Joan and five from me didn't add up to ten in Jenny: they added up to 110, with Jenny providing the other 100.

She was simply a perfect Jenny, and as Dr. Seuss told her: "There is no one alive who is you-er than you!" We hoped she would feel that way every day.

A Giving Child

THE CHASE WAS ON.

Joan and I had Jenny on the floor, with her pajamas unsnapped and half off, and we were trying to get a dry diaper on her. She'd twist and turn, rock and kick, and wriggle out of our grasp.

Then she was off across the rug, speed-crawling toward her stance in front of the stereo set. I was in pursuit, diaper in hand, Joan following closely. My mom and dad, visiting for Jenny's birthday, shouted encouragement from the sidelines while my dad snapped pictures.

Joan and I corralled Jenny as she was about to scoot under a table, but this was a job for one good man. I wrestled her into my lap, got the diaper on as quickly as I could, any which way I could, and closed up the Velcro tabs on the diaper cover. Jenny now was about to leap out of my lap. Breathing hard, my energy spent, I handed Jenny over to Joan to begin her bedtime routine.

"It's amazing how a child that small can defeat you," Joan said with a laugh. "But she does. Often."

Why was this small child so indomitable? Because she was holding nothing back. She gave everything she had. Every ounce of her went into whatever she did, from playing "peek-a-boo" to thwarting diaper changes.

If this all-out effort could exasperate us at times, we also knew it was a gift. What if we could maintain that intense involvement from our childhood, throwing everything we had into everything we did—and delighting in it? No reserve, no coolness, just complete exuberance and total absorption.

It was a gift to see that energy radiating from a child, especially during the holiday season. Each morning when we brought Jenny downstairs, her eyes would widen, her mouth would open, and she'd point with delight to the Christmas tree.

Jenny was with us when we picked out our little tree. She was fascinated when we put it up on a table in the living room—high enough so we wouldn't have to keep pulling her away from it. She was entranced a few days later when I put her in the backpack and worked on stringing the lights. Turning on the tree lights became an anticipated event each day.

But Jenny brought her own glow to this season of gathering and sharing. She loved being with people, and she delighted the people around her. We had a giving child.

Her giving began in small ways. When we were feeding her, she would always offer us some of her food. She would hold up her rice cake, or dip her spoon into her dinner, and offer to feed us. Sharing made her happy.

But her greatest gift always was giving of herself to other people. She watched, she listened, she paid attention. She showed her enjoyment, and her affection. If she wasn't tired or hungry or overwhelmed by the sheer scope of a gathering, she would invariably find some way to be delighted and to delight others—with laughter, smiles, babbling, or funny faces.

This happy, outgoing child was the same one who was so inconsolable through most of her first six months, who resisted being held, who cried so long with her angry little fists shaking beside her pained, reddened face. Seeing her deep distress in those difficult times, we sometimes wondered how much and how long we could keep giving.

But we never considered holding anything back from her. We accepted this principle from Dr. William Sears, on nurturing a high-need baby: "The intense baby may become the creative child; the sensitive infant, the compassionate child. The little 'taker' may later become a big giver." Whatever we gave Jenny in this first year, we were receiving greater gifts from her each day. She became a big giver indeed.

As she grows and learns more about the world, she will see the emphasis placed on getting and taking, particularly at this time of the year. Before long, she will be focusing her all-out efforts on accumulating all the items on her wish list, ranging from books to Barbie dolls (as long as it isn't too big a list). We can look forward to Jenny's delight in tearing open her presents and bounding from one toy to another. It will be a normal development for a child, though dealing with her wants will be different from dealing with her needs.

Will she understand that important difference? Will she see the value of giving? And as she comes to learn about receiving gifts, will she remain a big giver? If she does, we know she will always be a special child, with her own special gift.

Remembering a Year and a Life

WHERE DID THE YEAR GO?

I could probably tell you exactly where it went, almost by the minute, by the tear, and by the smile.

In an interview on National Public Radio, novelist John Updike said writing a book "is a little like childbirth. You tend to forget the pain and just enjoy the product." And no wonder, with such a precious product. Forgetting pain is a natural reaction, a natural defense. In the early, burned-out part of that first year with Jenny, someone told me: "Don't worry, you'll forget all about these times." Sounds reasonable: who would want to relive pain or hardship?

Me, that's who.

The first year I spent as an at-home father represented the hardest work I'd ever done, and the best. I wanted to remember every detail, every emotion from Jenny's first year, from the most difficult struggle to the most intoxicating joy. I wanted permanent images of the nights of tears, like the night Jenny cried in my arms for seven hours. I wanted detailed portraits of her first smile, at twenty-two days old; of her first laugh, at twelve weeks; of every little hurt and happiness we all felt.

I knew it couldn't be done, not in such minute detail, not even with a journal. But we enjoy the product so much more completely if we try to remember as much as we can of its production. Remembering is a step toward understanding, and understanding is a source of power in our lives. Most importantly, understanding can make a crucial difference in our children's lives.

Our children might be a lot better off if we remember—and admit—how difficult it can be to give them the care and understanding they need. At times, we may even wonder if we have any more to give. But I think we could appreciate ourselves more fully if we remember the effort we put into being parents, especially in the early days. Our connections to our children could not help but benefit.

If I didn't remember the long days and nights of pain and crying, if I hadn't tried to understand what Jenny was feeling, I could not have taken such delight in her laughter. If I had not held her on my shoulder and tried to draw the hurt out of her tense little body, I could not have appreciated the gifts of the playful happiness in her eyes, her smiles, and her kisses. They were flowers in the rain.

Remembering that year, and seeing the smiling and exuberant outcome, Joan and I were sure we understood this much: if we had held anything back from Jenny, we might have cost her the chance for her happiness. We focused on her needs, not on our convenience—or anyone else's convenience, for that matter.

And the result: we wanted to say to the world, "Look at that smile!"

Jenny's smile is the right start for a life. Her smile is the future, and the future never felt so tangible, so immediate. Joan and I have a wondrous child who is growing into that future, and we'll be growing along with her.

New parents can often feel they have given up their life when a baby arrives. And it's true: that old life is left at the bottom of a pile of dirty diapers. But if you want an education in life, then have a child—and try to understand that child. Because to do so you must understand yourself first.

I spent that first year with Jenny uncovering who I am and reinventing myself. Altering the patterns of half a lifetime, when work and travel were full-time escapes, I found new strength in giving and nurturing. Changing my life was not easy, but I had never lived every moment as intensely as I did during that year, because I had never examined every moment so closely.

The one clear lesson I learned: my problems were my own. They were all within myself. Feelings were natural and inevitable, no matter how difficult. But I could either choose to deal with them, and treat them as issues to be understood and settled; or I could turn them into dark and recurring problems by denying them or disowning them, and foment confrontations by blaming them on someone else.

Anger and impatience were my biggest hindrances, but they could usually be traced to ignoring what was going on inside me, ignoring the warning signs from the little grinding wheels and gears that needed to be oiled. My adversary was not a crying baby or a tired wife; my adversary was the person inside me who was dishonest about what was going on and about what I was feeling.

Face the questions and deal with them, or ignore the questions and suffer with them: a simple lesson, but not an easy one to learn, and not an easy one to live. But the lessons must go on, if we want to continue living.

As we reached the end of Jenny's first year, Joan and I were anticipating some pretty wonderful lessons. We were about to meet a walking, talking child with a boundless capacity for learning, and for teaching—about her life and ours. I always knew Jenny would be an earnest little pupil; but I also found her to be a wise and gifted little teacher, as this journal should show in every page.

Jenny may already have taught me more than I can ever teach her, and I still have so much to learn, as a father and as a man. I'll be depending on her.

Epilogue

July 1992

I ALWAYS HOPED that the time I've spent with Jenny would produce a unique relationship for us, and I think it has. I always hoped that Jenny would see me as a special kind of father, and I think she does.

In fact, she said so one day. As we completed the 5,123rd diaper change of my two-and-a-half years as an at-home father, Jenny smiled up at me, patted me on the arm, and said, "You're a good Mommy, Daddy."

What a kid.

When Jenny was sixteen months old, Joan and I took her to a nearby park to see some of the early flowering trees of springtime. We were looking at a magnolia when a petal fell into Jenny's hand. She studied it and held it. And when it was time to go, she refused to leave the park until Joan and I brought her back to the magnolia tree. She wanted to put back the petal.

What a kid.

For months, Jenny would awaken each morning, sit up in bed, and perk up her ears. Her first words would be: "What's that noise?" And she'd ask that question countless times during the day: "What's that noise?" She wanted to identify every sound—and she can hear an astounding range of them.

Several times, she has startled me by saying, "Somebody's at the door" an instant before I heard the bell or a knock. Her hearing is so acute, she heard the gate open and heard someone on our front walk before I had heard anything. She has saved me from missing several phone calls by saying: "Ringing! Telephone, Daddy!"

No doubt she inherited her "super hearing" from Joan, who arrived home from work one day, sat down on the couch with Jenny, and then dispatched me to find the source of a faint but insistent "beep-beep-beep" she was hearing. I couldn't find it; I couldn't hear it. But at six the next morning, we found out what it was: the tiny wake-up call of a small clock in the third-floor bathroom. Its alarm switch had been jostled into the "on" position. Joan had heard it from two floors away.

Jenny is fascinated by anything that makes noise. She'll jump at the chance to see a lawnmower the way most children jump at the chance to see a puppy. The more we see of Jenny's sensitivity to her environment, the more we're certain it played a major role in her discomfort during those early months: she couldn't shut out the world when she needed to.

Jenny seems to have inherited Joan's communication skills and "people" skills, but she's also curious about what goes on inside things, which she may have gotten from me. She'll get annoyed if she can't open up a toy to see what's inside and how it works.

Which leads us to an inevitable question we'll be facing surprisingly soon: what do we do about her education? How soon do we start her in preschool, and what kind of schooling do we select? Joan and I know we're going to have high standards for Jenny's school environment. We'll want excellent and patient teachers with small classes, where Jenny can count on encouragement and individual attention. (We'll also need teachers who will be able to cope with our high degree of involvement in her schooling.)

We know Jenny has good language skills, but we can't tell too much at this age about her mathematics skills. She has a mixed bag of math inheritance from her parents: I lasted through college calculus, but Joan began tuning out math when she reached plane geometry.

But if that's Jenny's greatest educational hurdle, we'll all be happy. Not that math is unimportant, but as Albert Einstein said: "Do not worry about your difficulties in mathematics; I can assure you that mine are still greater."

It's hard for us to imagine any serious limits on the capabilities of this eager and personable child, because it's almost impossible to keep her from learning.

Like Joan, Jenny has a library of emotions, and she's always ready to empty the shelves. But also like Joan, Jenny has an unusual awareness of her own emotional state, and an unusual sensitivity to the emotional state of those around her. If one of us seems a bit out of focus, Jenny is often the first to say "What's wrong with Daddy?" or "What's wrong with Mommy?" And if Jenny is feeling out of focus, she prompts us to ask her: "What's wrong with Jenny?"

She did just that one morning, leaning over to Joan in bed and saying with a sad face: "What's wrong with Jenny?" As always, Joan responded with concern: "Poor sweetheart! What's wrong with Jenny?"

Jenny's face lit up and she began laughing. "Jenny's HAPPY!" she said, wiggling with glee.

If you can keep a child like that out of your arms, you're a better man than I am. But I can't think of any episode that made us prouder of Jenny, or showed more of the kind of child she had become, than an incident at our neighborhood playground when Jenny was approaching two-and-a-half.

A little boy about her age was at the playground with his mom. But he had been born several weeks prematurely, so his development had not quite caught up to his chronological age.

The little boy was sitting atop one of Jenny's favorite pieces of equipment: a slide with two lanes. He was perched at the edge but he was afraid to slide down. He began to cry softly. Jenny, who had climbed up and sat down next to him, looked at him and reached for his hand. He wouldn't give it to her, but she kept trying and finally he relented. She sat at the top of the slide with him, quietly holding his hand.

What a kid.

Some things have changed, some have not. Jenny now has a sitter who is in our home with her most days from nine to five while I work upstairs and try to keep the house running. Between her journeys out into the world, Jenny will come bounding into my office with a "Hi, Daddy!" and climb up on my lap to type on the computer keyboard. She and her new pal are nuts about each other and keep each other energized. I guess I'm now more of a "supervisor daddy" during the day, but I'm still home and seldom more than a shout away. And there are still plenty of opportunities for a "sneak attack" to get Jenny giggling.

We've maintained our "attachment" style of parenting, holding her, comforting her, supporting her, and respecting her. We've never spent "quality time" with her; we've given her virtually all the time we've had to give. We've taken the road less traveled, and we believe it has made all the difference with Jenny.

That's not to say she isn't a normal two-year-old. She's not above some high-pitched chanting of "NO! NO! NO! NO! NO!" when some request meets her disapproval. But this is a fun kid: bright and happy, with big green eyes and a captivating smile. And most often, her words are rewards. After a summer Sunday spent visiting her grandmother on Chicago's North Side, romping in the playground across the street, and seeing the animals at the Lincoln Park Zoo and the flowers in the conservatory, a tired Jenny told me what was on her mind as I kissed her good night.

"I had a wonderful day, Daddy," she said.

So did I, Jenny. Every day.

Other Noble Press Books

THE DOCTOR, THE MURDER, THE MYSTERY
The True Story of the Dr. John Branion Murder Case
Barbara D'Amato

A gripping story of justice tragically miscarried, written by acclaimed mystery writer Barbara D'Amato.

"D'Amato . . . writes dispassionate nonfiction with objectivity and an overriding sense of fairness. Anyone wrongly convicted of a major crime would want to beg, borrow or steal to get her to look into the case. She is highly skilled in the tricky craft of journalism." *Chicago Sun-Times*
$20.95, hardback, 319 pages

GOING OFF THE BEATEN PATH
An Untraditional Travel Guide to the U.S.
Mary Dymond Davis

"A stimulating journey down the back roads and byways of the nation's active environmental movement." *Los Angeles Times*

"An exhaustive descriptive catalog . . . for those cynical moments when one doubts that anything ever changes." *Utne Reader*
$15.95, paperback, 468 pages

ECO-WARRIORS
Understanding the Radical Environmental Movement
Rik Scarce

An in-depth look at the people, the actions, the history, and the philosophies behind such groups as Earth First!, The Sea Shepherds, Greenpeace, and the Animal Liberation Front.

". . . intriguing, if sometimes disturbing reading . . . a fine account for anyone looking for insight into the environmental movement." *New York Times Book Review*
"Warning! Potent ideas at work." *Bloomsbury Review*
"[A] good and honest book that tells about an important social movement." *San Francisco Chronicle*
$12.95, paperback, 320 pages

EMBRACING THE EARTH
Choices for Environmentally Sound Living
D. Mark Harris

A practical guide on how to turn every day into an Earth Day. Contains over 200 do-able projects to begin living more lightly on the Earth. Charmingly illustrated and gently persuasive.

"This book is not only a call to action, it is the guide you need to act." *East West*
"Embracing the Earth encourages us to live an environmentally sound lifestyle 365 days a year [and] Harris makes you want to." *South Carolina Wildlife*
$9.95, paperback, 164 pages

HANDLE WITH CARE
A Guide to Responsible Travel in Developing Countries
Scott Graham

Practical guide on how to travel responsibly in such countries as India, Peru, and Mexico, among others. *Handle With Care* shows the traveller how to help preserve the natural environment, observe local customs, support the local economy, and find responsible tour groups.

$8.95, paperback, 168 pages

POISONING OUR CHILDREN
Surviving in a Toxic World
Nancy Sokol Green

Suggestions on how to rid your home of the deadly toxic chemicals that are a part of all our lives, by a woman suffering from Environmental Illness.

$12.95, paperback, 270 pages

PICTURE THIS!
A Guide to Over 300 Environmentally, Socially, and Politically Relevant Films and Videos
Sky Hiatt

Reviews of movies that address such subjects as racism, poverty, environmental destruction, political oppression, and animal cruelty, among others. Movies reviewed include *The Atomic Cafe, All Quiet on the Western Front, Mississippi Burning,* and *Drugstore Cowboy.*

$12.95, paperback, 398 pages

TWENTYSOMETHING, FLOUNDERING, AND OFF THE YUPPIE TRACK
A Self-Help Guide to Making It Through Your Twenties
Steven Gibb

A practical but humorous look at how to make the most out of one of the most difficult periods in life, by a twentysomething psychologist. Chapters include Leaving the Beer Kegs Behind, Finding Meaningful Work, How to Survive on $14,000 a Year, Moving in With Mom and Dad—Again.

$10.95, paperback, 176 pages

FREE THE ANIMALS
The Untold Story of the U.S. Animal Liberation Front and its Founder, "Valerie"
Ingrid Newkirk

The shattering account of one woman's underground struggle against the forces supporting abuse of animals, as told to America's foremost animal rights advocate.

"A moving story about extreme cruelty and extreme courage, and an inspirational and practical guide for anyone bent on challenging the system." *Oliver Stone*

$13.95, paperback, 372 pages

ECO-JOURNEYS
The World Guide to Ecologically Aware Travel and Adventure
Stephen Foehr
A one-of-a-kind comprehensive reference guide to travel and recreation around the world that promotes ecological awareness and participatory, hands-on adventure. Designed for environmentally conscious travelers everywhere, and written by an award-winning veteran travel writer who has lived and worked in over eighty countries.
$14.95, paperback, 310 pages

THE PSYCHOLOGY OF WAR
Comprehending its Mystique and its Madness
Lawrence LeShan
From best-selling psychologist and thinker Lawrence LeShan, a path-breaking consideration of war as an aspect of human experience.
"Rich with insight, and so compelling I could not put it down. How good it would be if every legislator and cabinet member read and took to heart the practical suggestions LeShan has for making peace planning as potent as war planning." *Hugh Downs*
$16.95, hardback, 163 pages

DEFENDING THE LEFT
An Individuals Guide to Fighting for Social Justice, Individual Rights, and the Environment
David E. Driver
An inspiring guidebook for progressive Americans who are ready to end the conservative assault on human rights, equal opportunity, and the environment, written by the author of *The Good Heart Book*. *Defending the Left* will show you what you can do to make the "Progressive Renaissance" of the nineties become a reality.
$11.95, paperback, 215 pages

All books are available from your local bookstore or directly from The Noble Press. Please add $2.00 for postage and handling for one book, $.50 for each additional book.

The Noble Press
213 W. Institute Place, Suite 508
Chicago, IL 60610
1-800-486-7737